Class Structure and Social Transformation

Class Structure and Social Transformation

Berch Berberoglu

Westport, Connecticut
London

Library of Congress Cataloging-in-Publication Data

Berberoglu, Berch.
    Class structure and social transformation / Berch Berberoglu.
      p.   cm.
    Includes bibliographical references and index.
    ISBN 0–275–94924–9 (alk. paper)
    1. Social conflict. 2. Social classes. 3. Social structure.
    I. Title.
    HM136.B378 1994
    305.5—dc20   94–12352

British Library Cataloguing in Publication Data is available.

Library of Congress Catalog Card Number: 94–12352
ISBN: 0–275–94924–9

First published in 1994

Praeger Publishers, 88 Post Road West, Westport, CT 06881
An imprint of Greenwood Publishing Group, Inc.

Printed in the United States of America

The paper used in this book complies with the
Permanent Paper Standard issued by the National
Information Standards Organization (Z39.48–1984).

10 9 8 7 6 5 4 3 2 1

Contents

Preface

Social classes and class structure are the most decisive forces that affect us in most everything we do in our lives. Human behavior varies in accordance with which class one belongs to and how one's class position and class consciousness translate into political action. An analysis of the class structure of society conveys the relationship between various social classes and how class relations and class conflict leads to an understanding of the class nature of social relations. A class analysis of society, therefore, is imperative for a clear understanding of the dynamics of class relations and class struggles.

Class means different things to different people; as the varied definitions and competing theories of class presented in the first and second chapters of this book make it clear, the critical factor that is decisive in the analysis of class structure is the definition one employs in conceptualizing class. Thus, while there exist a multiplicity of class definitions in the major theories of stratification and class structure, the definition used throughout this volume is that provided by historical materialism. In this sense, class is defined as an organic expression of social relations of production—relations that are lodged in the social-economic structure of society based on ownership and/or control of the means of production and, by extension, control of the state.

This book addresses many of the questions raised on the nature and dynamics of class structure and social transformation in comparative historical perspective. It also brings to focus the centrality of class in the analysis of society and social structure. Thus, the volume provides a concise statement of the decisive role played by class in shaping the contours of social life through time and across different societies—one that has an enormous impact on society and social relations on a world scale.

Acknowledgments

This book grew out of the need for a comprehensive yet concise analysis of class structure and social transformation that would provide the essentials of class analysis in comparative historical perspective. Given the macrosociological and historical scope of this undertaking which is the culmination of many years of research and study of the dynamics of class struggle and social change, the information provided in the following pages is a product of the contributions of scholars who have promoted a world view that stresses the centrality of class in social life, and the center stage that class struggle occupies in explaining social change and social transformation throughout history.

My interest in class analysis crystallized at the University of Oregon in the mid 1970s, where I did my advanced graduate work in sociology under the late Albert Szymanski. His approach to the study of society and social structure provided me with the foundations of class analysis based on the theoretical and methodological principles of dialectical and historical materialism. It is in this context of my advanced graduate studies that I came to adopt a definition of class based on social relations of production and arrived at the view based on a class analysis approach informed by this definition. For his crucial role in the formation of my thoughts on this question, I express my intellectual debt and gratitude to my mentor, friend, and colleague Al Szymanski.

Others who have also influenced my thinking on matters concerning the class nature of social relations and society in general include Larry Reynolds, Blain Stevenson, James Petras, Maurice Zeitlin, Paul Sweezy, Bill Warren, Goran Therborn, Nicos Poulantzas, Louis Althusser, Guglielmo Carchedi, Erik Olin Wright, and others. While I may not entirely agree with the approach taken by one or another of these theorists, they and many others have collectively contributed to the discussions and debates that have in different ways informed my views of class structure, class struggle, and social transformation.

More recently, numerous other individuals have, directly or indirectly, played an important role in the formation of my views on matters related to class. They include Walda Katz Fishman, Jim Salt, Martha Gimenez, John Leggett, Alvin So, Carla Filosa, Gianfranco Pala, and Alan Spector, to name a few. I would like to thank these and many other friends and colleagues who have discussed with me on numerous occasions many of the issues examined in this book.

Finally, I would like to thank my editor Jim Ice for his generous assistance in every stage of the publication process and to the reference librarians of the University of Nevada, Reno and the University of California, Berkeley for providing valuable assistance over the past number of years.

Prepared as a text for courses in social stratification at the advanced under-graduate level and for seminars in class structure at the graduate level, this book is dedicated to all those interested in studying class structure and class struggle and to those struggling to abolish all forms of exploitation, especially the exploitation of one class by another.

Introduction

The analysis of class structure and social transformation is the foundation of the macrosociological study of society in comparative historical perspective. An examination of the origins, development, and contradictions of social classes and class struggles over historical time and across national boundaries has been a preoccupation of social scientists concerned with social inequality and the impact of class on the structure and dynamics of societies around the world. Thus, the analysis of social classes and class structure constitutes the heart of the study of the structure and organization of society and social systems.

The process of transformation of societies from one social system to another depends on the nature and dynamics of class relations and class struggles that are historically specific in accordance with a society's dominant mode of production and its attendant superstructure. The study of the class structure of historical and contemporary societies, therefore, would inform us of the nature and dynamics of these societies and their transformation over time as determined by the level of development of their class contradictions.

The intensification of class struggles in a given social formation accelerates the resolution of the contradictions of a given mode of production through the revolutionary transformation of dominant relations of production. This in turn opens the way for an all-out struggle to transform social relations in general—a struggle that inevitably leads to a political rebellion to capture state power. The revolutionary overthrow of the ruling class of a decaying social system brought about by the unfolding class contradictions at the political level thus facilitates the emergence of a new social order. This process results in the development of society along the historical path to more advanced modes of production based on new and yet untested social relations which in time go through a similar cycle of dialectical resolution—a cycle that continues until the revolutionary transformations effected by class struggles come to an end at the highest stage of human social development.

This book attempts to address these and other related questions concerning the nature and structure of class relations in society in comparative historical perspective. The first two chapters take up the theoretical issues that are hotly debated among scholars who adhere to competing theoretical perspectives ranging from structural-functionalism, to elite theory, to Marxism.

In Chapter 1, I examine the major conventional theories of stratification and inequality, including functionalism, elite theory, Weberian theory, and various institutional theories of power and social inequality. After an extended analysis of their main arguments and assumptions, I provide a critique of these theories for either failing to address the real *class* forces beneath broader social relations or for falling short of an analysis of classes that would identify the key actors in unequal power relations. I argue that while these theories identify institutional processes that appear to wield power, in reality they are the manifestations of class relations based on relations of production.

In Chapter 2, I present an alternative theory of class inequality based on the historical materialist approach advanced by classical Marxism. Here I provide an in-depth analysis of the relationship between the social-economic base (or foundation) of society and the political superstructure in delineating the relationship between class and state. In examining this relationship, I argue that the class structure of society and the balance of class forces determine the nature and role of the state as an agent of class rule for the domination of one class by another. In this context, I show that the transformation of class relations also involves at the same time the transformation of the state as an instrument of force and the domination of the exploited class, and of society in general, on behalf of the propertied ruling classes. The overthrow of the state by the exploited masses, therefore, takes on political content when they rise up against not only unjust economic conditions, but also the political power that sustains and protects the interests of the wealthy and privileged classes. The correlation of forces that bring about simultaneously a political *and* a social revolution thus opens the way to the transformation of society onto the next stage of social development in history.

In Chapter 3, I examine the historical development of class systems from earlier times to the present. Tracing the process of social transformation throughout human history, I examine the nature, dynamics, and contradictions of primitive communal, despotic, slave-owning, feudal, and capitalist societies. I show that in the later stages of primitive communal society a social surplus emerged which led to the development of social classes and class struggles. The rise of a privileged class in the transition from primitive communal to early forms of class society led at the same time to the emergence of the state as an institution to protect and advance the interests of the dominant class. The Oriental despotic state thus came to represent the first developed form of the state as protector of the interests of a privileged bureaucratic elite emerging out of the primitive commune—an elite that became consolidated into a mature ruling class with the practice of slavery as the dominant mode of production. In time, slavery gave way to feudalism and subsequently to capitalism, such that the main forms of class society became identified as those based on the exploitation of slaves, serfs, and wage laborers under the slave-owning, feudal, and capitalist systems, respectively.

In Chapter 4, I examine the class structure of capitalist society, focusing on its advanced, contemporary stages of development and contradictions. A society based on the exploitation of wage labor for private profit, the class structure of capitalism reveals the struggle between labor and capital as the decisive, defining characteristic of the system and its contradictions.

In Chapter 5, I shift the focus of analysis to the periphery of the world capitalist system and examine the class structure of Third World societies in Latin America, Asia, Africa, and the Middle East. Tracing their colonial history and class structure over the past several centuries, I examine the nature and contradictions of class relations in these societies that are in transition to higher stages of social-economic development characterized by capitalist relations of production.

An important aspect of class relations that in the age of imperialism has become increasingly important throughout the world is nationalism. In Chapter 6, I take up the question of the relationship between class, nation, and state and examine the class nature of nationalism and national movements. I argue that although class relations and class struggles lie at the heart of nationalism and the national question, the recent upsurge in such movements makes it imperative to study the social origins and class nature of these phenomena, for without the resolution of the national question we cannot make progress toward the resolution of class antagonisms and class struggles and expect a revolutionary rupture that would move society toward a higher level of development based on an egalitarian social order that has overcome divisions along national and class lines.

The relationship between race, gender, and class is another important component of the analysis of class structure and social transformation. I take up this question for study in Chapter 7. Focusing on the debates surrounding class, gender, and race, I examine the relationship between these phenomena by focusing on the works of a number of theorists who address these questions. Through a critical presentation of their arguments, I show that while race and gender are, like nationalism, important phenomena that affect class relations and class struggles, to understand their nature and role in contemporary capitalist society, one must situate them in the proper context of class relations that define the totality of social structure including gender and race.

The book concludes with reference to the relationship between class struggle, revolution, and social transformation, pointing out that large-scale transformation of social relations at the societal level cannot take place without a thorough transformation of the existing class structure. Such transformation is possible only through the resolution of the class contra-dictions imbedded in the existing social order—contradictions that inevita-bly lead to the overthrow of the ruling class and the state and other superstructural institutions of society. The transformation of the old order and the emergence of a new one, I argue, thus depends on the degree of success of the class forces struggling to effect change in a new, egalitarian direction, and it is only through such change that society can finally free itself from the contradictions that define the nature of social life affected by class.

We begin our study with a critical analysis of competing mainstream theories of social class and inequality, followed by an examination of the Marxist theory of class structure and class struggle. The remainder of the book addresses the theoretical issues raised in the early chapters by apply-ing the concepts of historical materialism to the study of society from earlier times to the present.

Class Structure and
Social Transformation

One

Theories of Social Class and Inequality: A Critical Analysis

This chapter provides a critical analysis of major mainstream theories of social class and inequality. The theories examined here are divided into several broad groupings which include the functionalist; Weberian; classical elite; and organizational and force theories of stratification, class, and inequality. A critical analysis of these theories will help us understand conventional approaches to social inequality and thus situate the alternative Marxist theory of class discussed in the next chapter in proper perspective.

We begin our analysis with the dominant paradigm among mainstream academics on society and social inequality—the functionalist theory—which until recently played a dominant role in the study of social class and inequality in American society.[1]

THE FUNCTIONALIST THEORY OF STRATIFICATION AND INEQUALITY

The modern functionalist view of society, as exemplified in the works of Talcott Parsons and others, is concerned with the relationship of the various parts to the social system as a whole. As each part or unit of the system is given equal importance, any change in one part will affect all the others. To maintain conditions of stability within the system, society must be in a state of "equilibrium"—one that promotes the survival and maintenance of the prevailing social system.[2] This is clearly evident in the functionalists' discussion of social stratification and inequality in society.

Generally, the functionalists see stratification and inequality as naturally occuring phenomena in all societies at all times. In their classic article "Some

Principles of Stratification" published in 1945, Kingsley Davis and Wilbert E. Moore set forth what they call "an effort . . . to explain, in functional terms, the *universal necessity* which calls forth stratification in *any* social system."[3]

The central thesis of the functionalist theory of inequality, as outlined by Davis and Moore, is the "universal functional necessity of stratification," transcending any and all temporal and structural properties of human societies in the historical development process. "The main functional necessity explaining the universal presence of stratification," they write, "is precisely the *requirement* faced by *any* society of placing and motivating individuals in the social structure."[4] The model set forth in this theory is based on the following premise:

As a functioning mechanism a society must somehow distribute its members in social positions and induce them to perform the duties of these positions. It must thus concern itself with motivation at two different levels: to instill in the proper individuals the desire to fill certain positions, and, once in these positions, the desire to perform the duties attached to them.[5]

Davis and Moore go on to argue,

It does make a great deal of difference who gets into which positions, not only because some positions are inherently more agreeable than others, but also because some require special talents or training and some are functionally more important than others.[6]

Talcott Parsons, in agreement with this formulation, asserts that "social stratification is regarded . . . as the differential ranking of the human individuals who compose a given social system and their treatment as superior and inferior to one another in certain socially important respects."[7] Similarly, stratification, argues another functionalist, is inevitable and is the result of the problem of societies to motivate their members to work hard to live up to social values.[8] This assertion, like other functionalist claims on this question, is based on the assumption that stratification is "functionally necessary" to ensure the socialization of "proper individuals" to develop the desire and the skills to occupy important, functionally specific positions that are "required" for the maintenance of the social system.

The social system is maintained, argue the functionalists, through the allocation of "variable rewards" so that the greater the skill requirements and the importance of the position the greater are the "rewards." The disproportionate distribution of rewards, the argument goes, is for the purpose of filling the appropriate positions that are "necessary" for the "proper functioning" of society. This point is made quite clear by Davis and Moore:

Inevitably, then, a society must have, first, some kind of rewards that it can use as inducements, and second, some way of distributing these rewards differentially according to positions. The rewards and their distribution become a part of the social order, and thus give rise to stratification.[9]

And, they continue, "if the rights and prerequisites of different positions in society must be unequal, then the society must be stratified."[10] This leads them to conclude that "social inequality is thus an unconsciously evolved device by which societies ensure that the most important positions are conscientiously filled by the most qualified persons."[11] This is so, according to Davis and Moore, in "every society, no matter how simple or complex."[12]

Viewed from a critical standpoint, the Davis-Moore theory poses a number of conceptual, theoretical, and empirical problems at the outset. At the conceptual level, it should be stated that the confusion over the definition of stratification is so widespread that it has created a controversy even between functionalists themselves. To the extent that stratification is taken to mean a ranking of positions or statuses along various social dimensions and the differential classification of these positions based on real or apparent differences between them, there would be no major disagreement as to the usefulness of such model as a classificatory scheme. However, problems do arise when the concept is turned into a tautology and is given universal and metaphysical properties, that is, "universality," "universal functional necessity," and "inevitability" of social inequality.

Providing a substantive critique of the various arguments raised by the Davis-Moore theory, Melvin M. Tumin, a functionalist himself, sets out to refute, in functional terms, the former's contentions on social inequality concerning the greater or lesser "functional importance" of various positions, the questions of "motivation" and "reward," and the "positive functionality" and "universality" hence "inevitability" of social inequality.[13] We cannot here go into an extended analysis of each one of these points, but it is interesting to note that Tumin's critical analysis of these issues leads him to reach almost exactly the opposite conclusions from those of Davis and Moore, as he specifies various "negative functions, or dysfunctions, of institutionalized social inequality," for example, "human ignorance, war, poverty."[14] Since Tumin identifies these as the negative consequences of systems based on social inequality, the "contribution" of stratification to the positive functioning of society, according to his reasoning, does in fact become "dysfunctional" for society or the social system as a whole.

Challenging the theoretical and methodological premises of the Davis-Moore thesis on the functional necessity of stratification and inequality, Tumin raises some important issues that must be noted:

Since a theoretical model *can* be devised in which all other clearly indispensable major social functions are performed, but in which inequality as motive and reward is absent, how then account for stratification in terms of structural and functional necessities and inevitabilities?[15]

Extending his analysis to account for the key mechanism that perpetuates structured social inequality, "an essential characteristic of all known kinship systems," writes Tumin,

is that they function as transmitters of inequalities from generation to generation. Similarly, an essential characteristic of all known stratification systems is that they employ the kinship system as their agent of transmission of inequalities.

To the extent that this is true, then it is true by definition that the elimination from kinship systems of their function as transmitters of inequalities (and hence the alteration of the definition of kinship systems) would eliminate those inequalities which were generation-linked.

Obviously, the denial to parents of their ability and right to transmit both advantages and disadvantages to their offspring would require a fundamental alteration in all existing concepts of kinship structure. At the least, there would have to be a vigilant separation maintained between the unit which reproduces and the unit which socializes, maintains and places. In theory, this separation is eminently possible. In practice, it would be revolutionary.[16]

Indeed it would! By curbing the transfer of wealth and property through altering the nature and function of the kinship structure, it is indeed possible to bring up a generation of individuals without the necessity of a significant level of social inequality.

It should be noted that the functionalist contention of "the universality of social stratification," to be found in "every society, no matter how simple or complex," stands in sharp contrast to the notion of historical specificity. While on the one hand this universal model of the functionalists helps to consolidate their position theoretically and ideologically—thereby eliminating the possibility of the differential development of social evolution—it also conflicts with empirical reality. "Functional theories," comments Arthur Stinchcombe, "are like other scientific theories: they have empirical consequences which are either true or false. Deciding whether they are true or false is not a theoretical or ideological matter but an empirical one."[17] As the wealth of data available on a vast number of primitive societies show, almost all (98%) of hunting and gathering societies studied by anthropologists confirm that these societies do not have a class system or structured social inequality,[18] while the remaining 2 percent have become "stratified" as a result of contact with more advanced societies.[19] Hence, as humans have lived in primitive hunting and gathering societies as the predominant form of social organization for most of human history, it is clear that the historical evolution of Homo sapiens for thousands of years has been unquestionably highly democratic and egalitarian. Only in more recent times do we begin to see stratification and class systems develop, hence we have class inequality.[20]

Critics of modern functionalism have pointed out that the functionalists, consciously or unconsciously, have accepted existing structures and conditions in capitalist society as given, and have thus contributed to maintaining the existing social order and perpetuating the dominant capitalist ideology. This has opened the way to a flood of criticism of modern functionalism as being, in effect, nothing more than an ideological expression of contemporary capitalist society.

THE WEBERIAN THEORY OF CLASS AND SOCIAL INEQUALITY

It is often pointed out by Weberian theorists that Weber's theory of stratification and inequality is "multidimensional." By this is meant Weber utilized a number of equally important dimensions of class and social status to explain social structure and social inequality.

To Weber, "a 'class' is any group of persons occupying the same class status" or situation.[21] "We may speak of a 'class,' " he wrote, "when (1) a number of people have in common a specific causal component of their life chances, in so far as (2) this component is represented exclusively by economic interests in the possession of goods and opportunities for income, and (3) is represented under the conditions of the commodity or labor markets."[22] Central to Weber's conceptualization of class is the notion of "life chances," by which he means "the kind of control or lack of it which the individual has over goods or services and existing possibilities of their exploitation for the attainment of receipts within a given economic order."[23]

In the original Weberian formulation of class, "class situation" is ultimately "market situation": "According to our terminology," Weber tells us, "the factor that creates 'class' is unambiguously economic interest, and indeed, only those interests involved in the existence of the 'market.' "[24]

One's "class situation," then, is expressed by one's access to "a supply of goods, external living conditions, and personal life experiences"—all of which are derivative of and determined by the amount of control one has and which is exercised in the acquisition of income within a particular economic order. In his later formulations of class, Weber stresses the importance of "property" as the key variable that sets the parameters of this control.

" 'Property' and 'lack of property,' " Weber argues, are "the basic categories of all class situations."[25] In this formulation, one's life chances are "primarily determined by the differentiation of property holdings" and power is derived from the ownership and control of property "which gives [the owners] a monopoly to acquire [highly valued] goods."[26] And since the specific life chances of individuals are created by "the way in which the disposition over material property is distributed, . . . this mode of distribution monopolizes the opportunities for profitable deals for all those who [possess property]."27

Although Weber's conception of "property" is somewhat different from the Marxist definition, and that consequently such conception necessarily alters the analytical boundaries of the Weberian definition of the nature, position, and politics of specific classes, it does nonetheless point to the centrality of property relations in the control and exercise of power in society.28

In addition to the "property class," which constitutes the determinant core of Weber's concept of class, Weber distinguishes two other classes that make up the totality of his class model: "acquisition class" and "social class."29

A class is an "acquisition class" when the class situation of its members is primarily determined by their opportunity for the exploitation of services on the market; the "social class" structure is composed of the plurality of class statuses between which an interchange of individuals on a personal basis or in the course of generations is readily possible and typically observable.30

While "acquisition classes" are based on occupational criteria, as opposed to property ownership, "social classes" are largely a product of the combination of occupational *and* property classes: the "working" class, the "lower middle" classes, the "intelligentsia," and "the classes occupying a privileged position through property and education."31

We cannot here go into a detailed description of each one of these classes, but suffice it to say that Weber, in the case of both property and acquisition classes, further subdivides them into "positively privileged" and "negatively privileged" classes and adds an intermediate category, making up the "middle class." As Weber puts it:

Positively privileged property classes typically live from property income. This may be derived from property rights in human beings as with slaveowners, in land, in mining property, in fixed equipment such as plant and apparatus, in ships, and as creditors in loan relationships. . . . Finally, they may live on income from securities.

Class interests which are negatively privileged with respect to property . . . are themselves objects of ownership, that is they are unfree [such as slaves].32

Similarly, "social status," according to Weber, rests on "a typically effective claim to positive or negative privilege with respect to social prestige" derived from "one or more of the following bases: *(a)* mode of living, *(b)* a formal process of education . . . and the acquisition of the corresponding, modes of life, or *(c)* on the prestige of birth, or of an occupation."33 Thus, within this framework, a social "*stratum*," then, "is a plurality of individuals who, within a larger group, enjoy a particular kind and level of prestige by virtue of their position."34 As Weber puts it elsewhere:

One might thus say that "classes" are stratified according to their relations to the production and acquisition of goods; whereas "status groups" are stratified according to the principles of their *consumption* of goods as represented by special "styles of life."[35]

And, as it is clear from Weber's repeated emphasis, *social status* is a manifestation of class situation, rooted in property relations, and thus is a derivative of *class* status.

Still, although control over wealth, income, goods, services, education, high official position, power, and other privileges in the hands of the "positively privileged" property class and lack of such control and appropriation on the part of the "negatively privileged" property class place Weber's analytic scheme in a position that is in a sense analogous to the Marxist conception of exploiting and exploited classes, the logic of such classification is based on an entirely different set of conceptual definitions that separate the two traditions.[36]

THE ELITE THEORY OF STRATIFICATION AND INEQUALITY

The elite theory of stratification maintains that all societies are ruled by elites and that the major institutions of society, especially the state, constitute the mechanism by which the vast majority is ruled. Classical elite theory, advanced by Vilfredo Pareto and Gaetano Mosca, argues that this is so because the masses are inherently incapable of governing themselves, and that therefore society must be led by a small number of individuals who rule on behalf of the masses.

In his major work, *The Mind and Society*, Vilfredo Pareto identified a minority of highly talented individuals at the top levels of society who possessed superior personal qualities and wielded great social and political power; distinguishing this group from the great masses of the people, Pareto called it the "*élite.*"[37] "So let us make a class of the people who have the highest indices in their branch of activity," wrote Pareto, "and to that class give the name of *élite.*"[38] Further elaborating on the internal composition of this group, he divided the elite into two (political and social) segments:

A *governing élite*, comprising individuals who directly or indirectly play some considerable part in government, and a *nongoverning élite*, comprising the rest. . . .

So we get two strata in a population: (1) a lower stratum, the *non-élite*, with whose possible influence on government we are not just here concerned; then (2) a higher stratum, *the élite*, which is divided into two: (*a*) a governing *élite*, (*b*) a nongoverning *élite*.[39]

Within this framework, the fundamental idea set forth and developed by Pareto was that of the "circulation of elites." By this, Pareto meant two diverse processes operative in the perpetual continuity of elite rule: (1) the process in which *individuals* circulate between the elite and the nonelite; and (2) the process in which a *whole elite* is replaced by a new one.

The main point of Pareto's concept of the circulation of elites is that the ongoing process of replenishing the governing elite by superior individuals from the lower classes is a critical element securing the continuation of elite rule.

The governing class is restored not only in numbers, but—and that is the more important thing—in quality, by families rising from the lower classes and bringing with them the vigor and the proportions of residues necessary for keeping themselves in power.[40]

A breakdown in this process of circulation of elites, however, leads to such serious instability in the social equilibrium that "the governing class crashes to ruin and often sweeps the whole of a nation along with it."[41]

In Pareto's reasoning, a "potent cause of disturbance in the equilibrium is the accumulation of superior elements in the lower classes and, conversely, of inferior elements in the higher classes."[42] Hence, "every *élite* that is not ready to fight to defend its position is in full decadence; there remains nothing for it to do but to vacate its place for another *élite* having the virile qualities which it lacks."[43]

Thus, Pareto reaches an inescapable conclusion in his four-volume study: "Aristocracies do not last. Whatever the causes, it is an incontestable fact that after a certain length of time they pass away. History is a graveyard of aristocracies."[44]

The consequences of developments in society are such that they eventually lead to total social transformation. According to Pareto,

Revolutions come about through accumulations in the higher strata of society . . . of decadent elements no longer possessing the residues suitable for keeping them in power, and shrinking from the use of force; while meantime in the lower strata of society elements of superior quality are coming to the fore, possessing residues suitable for exercising the functions of government and willing enough to use force.[45]

Pareto's explanation of the nature and dynamics of elite rule and their circulation, therefore, rests in large part on the personal qualities of individuals in both elite and nonelite segments of society and their willingness or failure to use force to acquire and retain political power.

Gaetano Mosca, the other major elite theorist, argued in his classic work *The Ruling Class* in favor of a theory of inequality and power similar to that advanced by Pareto. Like Pareto, he divided people in all societies into essentially two distinct classes: the ruling class (the elite) and the class that is ruled (the masses). The ruling class always enjoys a monopoly of political power over the masses and directs society according to its own interests:

In all societies . . . two classes of people appear—a class that rules and a class that is ruled. The first class, always the less numerous, performs all political functions, monopolizes power and enjoys the advantages that power brings, whereas the second, the more numerous class is directed and controlled by the first, in a manner that is now more or less legal, now more or less arbitrary and violent.[46]

This is not merely so with every known society of the past and the present; *all* societies *must* be so divided. Herein lies Mosca's argument for the "universal necessity" and "inevitability" of elite rule:

Absolute equality has never existed in human societies: Political power never has been, and never will be, founded upon the explicit consent of majorities. It always has been, and it always will be, exercised by organized minorities, which have had, and will have, the means, varying as the times vary, to impose their supremacy on the multitudes.[47]

Mosca attempts here to establish "the real superiority of the concept of the ruling, or political, class," to show that "the varying structure of ruling classes has a preponderant importance in determining the political type, and also the level of civilization, of the different peoples."[48] Hence for Mosca it is the political apparatus of a given society and an organized minority (i.e., the political elite) that controls this apparatus—not the class structure—that determines the nature and movement of society and societal change.[49]

At one point, Mosca writes that "the discontent of the masses might succeed in deposing a ruling class," but, he immediately adds, "inevitably . . . there would have to be another organized minority within the masses themselves to discharge the functions of a ruling class."[50] As Mosca viewed the specific "functions" of ruling classes in universal terms, he could not envision a state and a society at the service of the laboring masses, as against a ruling class or an "organized minority within the masses."

Mosca's tautological arguments on the "inevitability" of elite rule as expressed above cast a heavy shadow on his work and call into question the accuracy of his observations.

Although Mosca believed that the ruling classes throughout history "owe their special qualities not so much to the blood in their veins as to their very particular upbringing,"[51] and recognized that "social position, family tradition, the habits of the class in which we live, contribute more than is commonly supposed to the greater or lesser development of the qualities mentioned,"[52] he nonetheless failed to address the social and political implications of his own position by rejecting the class-struggle analysis of Marx and opting instead for a psychological theory of power based on an individualistic conception of human nature.

Given its contempt for the masses and its acceptance of elite rule over them as an inevitable outcome of social life, classical elite theory advanced by Pareto and Mosca lends itself to reactionary conclusions that have important political implications with respect to both the nature of social inequality and the prospects for social transformation in modern society.

More recently, a new stream of critical elite theorists led by C. Wright Mills shifted the focus of analysis onto the power structure, arguing that power lies in the hands of the chief administrators of national policy who collectively represent the overall interests of what Mills called "the power elite."

Influenced by the analysis provided by classical elite theory but rejecting its conservative, aristocratic assumptions about elites and masses, Mills in his pioneering work *The Power Elite* presented the core of his argument this way:

Within American society, major national power now resides in the economic, the political, and the military domains. . . . As each of these domains has coincided with the others, as decisions tend to become total in their consequence, the leading men in each of the three domains of power—the warlords, the corporation chieftains, the political directorate—tend to come together, to form the power elite of America.[53]

"The power elite," Mills went on to point out, is composed of those who are "in command of the major hierarchies and organizations of modern society." "They rule the big corporations. They run the machinery of the state and claim its prerogatives. They direct the military establishment. They occupy the strategic command posts of the social structure. . . ."[54] Mills also points out "this triangle of power is now a structural fact, and it is the key to any understanding of the higher circles in America today."[55]

The central point in Mills's analysis of the power elite is not the mere identification of the elite in the three key institutions that constitute the American power structure but the interrelationship between these institutions and between the members of the elite that control and direct them. Thus: "The shape and meaning of the power elite today can be understood only when these three sets of structural trends are seen at their point of coincidence."[56] According to Mills, the interrelationship between these institutions and between their top leadership is such that retired generals become corporate executives and serve on the boards of directors of large corporations that sell inflated military hardware through lucrative defense contracts signed by old associates in the military, while corporate executives who enter politics serve the interests of big business once they hold key government posts that facilitate the passage of legislation favorable to corporate interests. Thus, as the linkage between big business and the government becomes consolidated, so too the control of the state by business interests becomes solidified.

In line with the increased influence over and control of the government by big business, Mills also saw the rise of the military and its more direct role and influence in political affairs. "In so far as the structural clue to the power elite today lies in the enlarged and military state," he wrote, "that clue becomes evident in the military ascendency."[57] Mills argued that, "as the United States has become a great world power, the military establishment has expanded, and members of its higher echelons have moved directly into diplomatic and political circles."[58] As a result, "the higher military have ascended to a firm position within the power elite of our time."[59] Thus the generals, Mills concluded, "are now more powerful than they have ever been in the history of the American elite; they have now more means of exercising power in many areas of American life which were previously civilian domains."[60]

Critics of Mills have pointed out that his exaggerated emphasis on the rise of the military has had a lopsided effect on his tripartite model of the power elite, and that, contrary to all appearances at the time, developments since 1960 have shown that the ascendancy of the military was not a new and independent phenomenon foisted upon society, but a result of the interests of the corporate elite that promoted the military and what Mills called "a military definition of reality."[61] Thus, as one critic has argued, "in his tripartite division of the wielders of control," Mills "tends to ignore the central depository of power—the financial overlords."[62]

THE ORGANIZATIONAL AND FORCE THEORIES OF POWER AND INEQUALITY

Following the general theoretical premises of classical elite theory, a number of theorists have elaborated on two particularly important aspects of power exercised by ruling minorities—political organization and military force—and have examined the relationship of these phenomena to stratification and inequality in society. The first, advanced by Robert Michels, has come to be known as the organizational theory of political power; the second, developed by Stanislav Andreski, is referred to as the force theory of power and inequality.

Robert Michels, one of the most influential theorists of political organization, stressed that the source of the problem of elite rule lies in the nature and structure of bureaucratic organization.[63] He argued that bureaucratic organization itself, irrespective of the intentions of the bureaucrats, results in the formation of an elite-dominated society. Thus, regardless of ideological ends, organizational means would inevitably lead to oligarchic rule: "It is organization which gives birth to the dominion of the elected over the electors, of the mandataries over the mandators, of the delegates over the delegators. Who says organization, says oligarchy."[64]

At the heart of Michels's theoretical model lie the three basic principles of hierarchy that take place within the bureaucratic structure of political organization: (1) the need for specialized staff, facilities, and, above all, leaders; (2) the utilization of such specialized facilities by leaders within these organizations; and (3) the psychological attributes of the leaders (i.e., charisma).

Michels argued that the bureaucratic structure of modern political parties or organizations gives rise to specific conditions that corrupt the leaders and bureaucrats in such parties. These leaders, in turn, consolidate the power of the party leadership and set themselves apart from the masses. "Even the purest of idealists who attains to power for a few years," he argued, "is unable to escape the corruption which the exercise of power carries in its train."[65] For Michels, this pointed to the conservative basis of (any) organization, since the *organizational form* as such was the basis of the conservatism, and this conservatism was the inevitable outcome of power attained through political organization. Hence, "political organization leads to power, but power is always conservative."[66]

Such corruption, emerging from organizational authority, argued Michels, also occurs at the individual level. Hence, to close the various gaps in his theory, Michels resorted to human-nature-based tautological arguments: Once a person ascends to the leadership level, he or she becomes a part of the new social setting to the extent that he would resist ever leaving that position.

The apathy of the masses and their need for guidance has as its counterpart in the leaders a natural greed for power. Thus the development of the democratic oligarchy is accelerated by the general characteristics of human nature. What was initiated by the need for organization, administration, and strategy is completed by psychological determinism.[67]

The argument here is that the leader consolidates power around the newly acquired condition and uses that power to serve personal interests, thus becoming increasingly distant from the masses. As Michels puts it: "He who has acquired power will almost always endeavor to consolidate it and to extend it, to multiply the ramparts which defend his position, and to withdraw himself from the control of the masses."[68]

In his book *Military Organization and Society*, sociologist Stanislav Andreski argues that the basic determinant of inequality in and between societies is power, and that this power is lodged in the control and use of military force.[69] "The possession of wealth gives power," writes Andreski, "but as soon as we enquire into the meaning of the word 'possession,' we see that the economic power is derivative. . . . The norms, legal or customary, which support this control constitute, therefore, the foundations of economic power."[70] He goes on to argue that "in societies where inequalities of wealth are extreme, the property of the rich is respected mainly because of the fear of punishment."[71] This is so, because "the ability to compel through the use or the threat of violence is an irreducible form of power, which can exist without being supported by anything else."[72] Thus the logic of his argument leads Andreski to conclude that whoever holds military power holds the key to the control and domination of society. And a society that is militarily more powerful is able to dominate other societies that are inferior militarily. Andreski writes:

It is not surprising that it is almost always those who wield the military power who form the supreme stratum of society. The pure plutocracy, that is to say the rule of the rich who do not control the military power, can only be a temporary phenomenon. Purely economic factors produce, no doubt, fluctuations in the height of stratification, but . . . the long-term trends are determined by the shifts of the locus of military power.[73]

Further developing his argument along these lines, Andreski introduces into his model another variable that is directly linked to the stratification scheme of a given society: the "military participation ratio" (M.P.R.). According to Andreski, the M.P.R. is a major determinant of social stratification and refers to "the proportion of militarily utilized individuals in the total population."[74] The greater the number of individuals participating in the military, the more egalitarian and democratic is the society. Moreover, "the influence of the changes in M.P.R. on stratification will be modified according to whether the warriors equip and maintain themselves or whether they are equipped, provisioned, and paid by the government."[75] The argument here is that the warriors who are self-equipped and self-maintained are "much more independent, much better able to enforce their claims," whereas "if they are equipped and maintained by the government they are, as a rule, also fitted into an army organized by the government and commanded by officers appointed by it."[76] Hence, "high M.P.R. will exert a stronger leveling influence," Andreski continues, "if the armed forces fall into the first category."[77] What this means is that societies whose armed forces are made up of self-equipped and self-maintained soldiers, and where a large number of people participate in the military, tend to be more egalitarian than societies that have specialized professional armies and centrally supplied, sophisticated armaments. Moreover, "the influence which the M.P.R. exerts on the span of social inequalities is further modified by another factor":

The degree of superiority of the armed forces over the unarmed populace depends in the first place on the quality of the armament: a machine-gun confers upon its possessors a much greater superiority over an unarmed crowd than a sword. Also, if the production of armaments can be undertaken only in large-scale establishments, it is impossible to prepare an uprising secretly. Swords or even rifles can be manufactured clandestinely but not tanks or bombers. We can say, therefore, that the predominance of the armed forces over the populace grows as the armament becomes more elaborate. This predominance can also be due, sometimes entirely, to the advantage of organization. . . . Generally, we may say that the helplessness of the populace against armed forces grows with the importance of organization.[78]

The ease with which the masses can be kept down, or what Andreski calls "the suppression facility," is a major determinant of social structure that tends to sharpen social inequalities: "it accentuates the effects of the low M.P.R. and counteracts the effects of the high."[79]

While Andreski's analysis makes an important contribution to our understanding of the relationship between military organization and society, critics have argued that his claim of military power as the determinant of stratification and inequality in society is basically flawed. Marxist theorists have argued, for example, that although military strength is important in influencing the nature and direction of a particular social order, force (or military power) does not have a logic of its own. Rather it is rooted in the economic, that is, productive, structure of society, and that the nature and organizational structure of the military itself is based on the logic and the level of development of the mode of production and of the economy in general.[80] Hence, according to this view, the military, as in the case of the polity, is dependent on and is the outcome of the productive mode lodged in the economic structure of society. The power of the military is very much dependent on the economy:

Money must be provided through the medium of economic production; and so once again force is conditioned by the economic order, which furnishes the resources for the equipment and maintenance of the instruments of force. But even that is not all. Nothing is more dependent on economic preconditions than precisely the army and navy. Their armaments, composition, organization, tactics, and strategy depend above all on the stage reached at the time in production and communications.[81]

Thus, the relative strength, technological structure, and organizational form of the military, these critics have argued, are inevitably the outcome of the historically specific mode of production in society.

To develop a more comprehensive understanding of the relationship between class, power, and inequality, and to examine the nature and source of power and domination in society, we turn in the next chapter to the Marxist analysis of class structure and class struggle—the main alternative to mainstream theories of stratification, class, and inequality.

NOTES

1. We refer here to the Parsonian variety of contemporary functionalism—often referred to as "structural functionalism"—since it has been this particular

branch of functionalist theory that has gained paradigmatic dominance in the United States during the post-World War II period. We shall hereafter use the term "functionalism" for short, always remembering that our reference is to that of "Parsonian structural functionalism."

2. See Talcott Parsons, *The Social System* (New York: Free Press, 1951).

3. Kingsley Davis and Wilbert E. Moore, "Some Principles of Stratification," *American Sociological Review* 10, no. 2 (April 1945), p. 242; emphases added.

4. Ibid.; emphases added.

5. Ibid.

6. Ibid., p. 243.

7. Talcott Parsons, *Essays in Sociological Theory*, rev. ed. (Glencoe, Ill.: Free Press, 1954), p. 69.

8. H. Johnson, *Sociology* (New York: Harcourt, Brace and Company, 1960), pp. 468–549.

9. Davis and Moore, "Some Principles of Stratification," p. 243.

10. Ibid.

11. Ibid.

12. Ibid.

13. Melvin M. Tumin, "Some Principles of Stratification: A Critical Analysis," *American Sociological Review* 18, no. 4 (August 1953).

14. Ibid., 394; Melvin M. Tumin, "Reply to Kingsley Davis," *American Sociological Review* 18, no. 6 (December 1953), p. 672.

15. Tumin, "Reply to Kingsley Davis," p. 672.

16. Ibid.

17. Arthur L. Stinchcombe, "Some Empirical Consequences of the Davis-Moore Theory of Stratification," *American Sociological Review* 28, no. 5 (October 1963), p. 808.

18. Gerhard Lenski, *Power and Privilege* (New York: McGraw-Hill, 1966).

19. Eleanor B. Leacock, "Introduction," to F. Engels, *The Origin of the Family, Private Property, and the State* (New York: International Publishers, 1972).

20. See Albert Szymanski, *Class Structure* (New York: Praeger, 1983), chap. 2.

21. Max Weber, *The Theory of Social and Economic Organization*, ed. and with an intro. by Talcott Parsons (New York: Free Press, 1964), p. 424.

22. Max Weber, *From Max Weber, Essays in Sociology*, trans., ed., and intro. by H. H. Gerth and C. Wright Mills (New York: Oxford University Press, 1967), p. 181.

23. Weber, *The Theory of Social and Economic Organization*, p. 424.

24. Weber, *From Max Weber*, p. 183.

25. Ibid., p. 182.

26. Ibid.

27. Ibid., pp. 181–82.

28. See Max Weber, *The Protestant Ethic and the Spirit of Capitalism* (New York: Scribner's, 1948). As we have pointed out earlier, in the Weberian approach classes, including "property classes," are defined in terms of one's "market situation" or position in society, whereas in Marxist theory class relations are based on social relations of production. See chapter 2 in this book.

29. Weber, *The Theory of Social and Economic Organization*, p. 424.

30. Ibid.

31. Ibid., p. 427.

32. Ibid., p. 425.

33. Ibid., p. 428.

34. Ibid., pp. 428–29.

35. Weber, *From Max Weber*, p. 193; emphasis in the original.

36. For further discussion on this point, see chapter 2 in this book.

37. Vilfredo Pareto, *The Mind and Society*, 4 vols., ed. Arthur Livingstone (New York: Harcourt, Brace and Company, 1935).

38. Ibid., vol. 3, p. 1423.

39. Ibid., pp. 1423–24.

40. Ibid., pp. 1430–31.

41. Ibid., p. 1431.

42. Ibid.

43. Ibid., vol. 1, p. 40.

44. Ibid., vol. 3, p. 1430.

45. Ibid., p. 1431.

46. Gaetano Mosca, *The Ruling Class* (New York: McGraw-Hill, 1939), p. 50.

47. Ibid., p. 326.

48. Ibid., p. 51.

49. Ibid., p. 329.

50. Ibid., p. 329.

51. Ibid., p. 62.

52. Ibid., p. 63.

53. C. Wright Mills, *The Power Elite* (New York: Oxford University Press, 1956), pp. 6, 9.

54. Ibid., p. 4.

55. C. Wright Mills, "The Structure of Power in American Society," in *Power, Politics, and People: The Collected Essays of C. Wright Mills*, ed. Irving Louis Horowitz (New York: Oxford University Press, 1963), p. 27.

56. Mills, *The Power Elite*, p. 276.

57. Ibid., p. 275.

58. Ibid., p. 202.

59. Mills, "The Structure of Power in American Society," p. 28.

60. Mills, *The Power Elite*, p. 202.

61. See G. William Domhoff and Hoyt B. Ballard, eds. *C. Wright Mills and the Power Elite* (Boston: Beacon Press, 1969); and G. William Domhoff, *The Higher Circles: The Governing Class in America* (New York: Vintage, 1971), p. 139.

62. Herbert Aptheker, *The World of C. Wright Mills* (New York: Marzani and Munsell, 1960), pp. 19–20.

63. Robert Michels, *Political Parties* (New York: Free Press, 1968).

64. Ibid., p. 365.

65. Ibid., p. 355.

66. Ibid., p. 333.

67. Ibid., p. 205.

68. Ibid., p. 206.

69. Stanislav Andreski, *Military Organization and Society* (Berkeley: University of California Press, 1968).

70. Ibid., p. 25.

71. Ibid.

72. Ibid.
73. Ibid., p. 26.
74. Ibid., p. 33.
75. Ibid., p. 34.
76. Ibid.
77. Ibid., p. 35.
78. Ibid.
79. Ibid., p. 36.
80. See Albert Szymanski, *Class Structure: A Critical Perspective* (New York: Praeger, 1983), pp. 606–9.
81. Frederick Engels, *Anti-Duhring* (New York: International Publishers, 1976), p. 185.

Two

The Marxist Theory of Class Structure and Class Struggle

This chapter examines the Marxist theory of class structure and class struggle. Providing an analysis of social classes and class struggles based on the exploitation of labor, Marx and Engels stressed that such an analysis must be placed within the framework of the dynamics of social change in the world historical process and that in this context the crucial task is to identify and examine the *primary motive force of social transformation* that defines the parameters of societal development: *class struggle*.

To understand the centrality of class struggle in the Marxist analysis of society and social structure, we must first briefly discuss the theoretical foundation of the Marxist approach—historical materialism.

HISTORICAL MATERIALISM

The starting point in Marx and Engels's analysis of society and social relations is recognizing human beings as the prime agents of material production—a process that forms the basis of production and reproduction of human existence. As they put it:

Life involves before everything else eating and drinking, a habitation, clothing and many other things. The first historical act is thus the production of the means to satisfy these needs, the production of material life itself.[1]

Hence, in the early stages of history, principal human needs were based on and centered in subsistence for the sustenance of life.

Through time, humans created and developed tools, skills, knowledge, and work habits—in short, the *forces of production*—to an extent that permitted, for the first time, the accumulation of surplus. Although in most of human history, for thousands of years, human beings lived in classless primitive-communal societies, the accumulation of a social surplus in the form of a surplus product gave rise to the emergence of classes in society. With the development of social classes and class inequality, there emerged historically specific social *relations of production*, or class relations, between those who produced the surplus and those who claimed ownership and control of that surplus (e.g., slaves vs. masters; serfs vs. landlords; wage laborers vs. capitalists). Marx and Engels pointed out that the forces of production (including the labor process at the point of production) and the social relations of production (class relations) together constitute a society's *mode of production*, or its social-economic foundation, defined as the way in which a society's wealth is produced and distributed—in short, the social-economic system (e.g., slavery, feudalism, capitalism).

Applying these concepts to history and examining the material conditions surrounding the production and reproduction process, in effect the very basis of life itself, Marx and Engels observed the following:

The way in which men produce their means of subsistence depends first of all on the nature of the actual means they find in existence and have to reproduce. This mode of production must not be considered simply as being the reproduction of the physical existence of the individuals. Rather it is a definite form of activity of these individuals, a definite form of expressing their life, a definite *mode of life* on their part. As individuals express their life, so they are. What they are, therefore, coincides with their production, both with *what* they produce and with *how* they produce. The nature of individuals thus depends on the material conditions determining their production.[2]

Engels, in a letter to Heinz Starkenburg, further explains the historical materialist outlook on society this way:

What we understand by the economic conditions which we regard as the determining basis of the history of society are the methods by which human beings in a given society produce their means of subsistence and exchange the products among themselves (in so far as division of labour exists). Thus the *entire technique* of production and transport is here included. According to our conception this technique also determines the method of exchange and, further, the division of products and with it, after the dissolution of tribal society, the division into classes also and hence the relations of lordship and servitude and with them the state, politics, law, etc.[3]

Once a class society emerges—in which the production process is firmly established, a surplus is generated, and social classes have developed—the relations of production (or class relations) become the decisive element defining the nature of the dominant mode of production, which in turn gives rise to the political *superstructure*, including first and foremost the state, as well as other political and ideological institutions that serve the interests of the propertied classes in society. Thus, the superstructure arises from and becomes a reflection of the dominant mode of production which reinforces the existing social order, notwithstanding the fact that the superstructure itself may influence or otherwise effect changes in favor of the long-term interests of the dominant classes in society.[4] As Marx points out:

In the social production of their life, men enter into definite relations that are indispensable and independent of their will, relations of production which correspond to a definite stage of development of their material productive forces. The sum total of these relations of production constitutes the economic structure of society, the real foundation, on which rises a legal and political superstructure and to which correspond definite forms of social consciousness.[5]

For Marx, then, the *relations of production*, that is, the "relationship of the owners of the conditions of production to the direct producers reveals the innermost secret, the hidden basis of the entire social structure, and with it ... the corresponding specific form of the state."[6] The relations of production, as the decisive element in the mode of production, together with the political superstructure which emerges from it, thus constitute the very basis of the analysis of social classes, class structure, class struggles, and social transformation, according to Marxism.

SOCIAL CLASS AND CLASS STRUGGLE

The focal point stressed by Marx and Engels in explaining social class and class struggle is that an analysis of property-based unequal social relations prevalent in the organization of material production in class society is the key to understanding the nature of a particular social order. The position of people in the production process, situated according to their relation to the ownership/control of the means of production, is viewed by Marx and Engels as the decisive element defining class relations. It is from these historically specific social relations of production that inequalities precisely arise and lead to class conflict and class struggles, that is, struggles for political power. Thus, referring to class society, "the history of all hitherto existing society," Marx and Engels point out, "is the history of class struggles."[7]

In capitalist society, for example, there are two main classes that relate to one another in the production sphere: capitalists (owners of capital) and workers (wage labor). The capitalist class owns the means of production and accumulates capital through the exploitation of labor. The working class does not own the means of production but instead uses its labor power to generate value for the capitalists as a condition for its survival. Capitalist society is thus mainly divided into these two groups:

The class of modern capitalists, owners of the means of social production and employers of wage-labor . . . [and] the class of modern wage-laborers who, having no means of production of their own, are reduced to selling their labor-power in order to live.[8]

Under capitalist production, while a portion of the value generated by labor is returned to it for subsistence (wages), a much greater portion goes to the capitalist in the form of surplus value (profits), which, accumulated over time, enhances the wealth and fortunes of the capitalist class vis-à-vis all other classes in society, especially the working class, in both relative and absolute terms.[9]

The accumulation of capital through this process of exploitation under capitalism thus results in disparities in wealth and income between labor and capital and eventually leads to conflict and struggle between the two classes, extending to realms beyond the production sphere itself. Hence, in this class struggle, write Marx and Engels,

oppressor and oppressed stood in constant opposition to one another, carried on an uninterrupted, now hidden, now open, fight, a fight that each time ended, either in a revolutionary reconstitution of society at large, or in the common ruin of the contending classes.[10]

Marx and Engels conceptualized class at three different yet related levels: economic, social, and political. The first of these is identified as the foundation of class analysis, class-in-itself (*Klasse-an-sich*). This refers to groups of people who relate to production in the same way, that is, those who have the same property relationships in the productive process (e.g., workers, peasants, landlords, capitalists). Structurally, then, *class-in-itself* is the logical outcome of the mode of production in all class societies.

At the next, sociological, level is what can be referred to as *social class*. A class-in-itself becomes a social class only when there is a close relationship between the members of a particular class. In this sense, industrial workers (the classic proletariat) constitute a social class in that not only do the members of this class interact in the productive process (in factories, under socialized conditions of production) but they also have a distinct culture, lifestyle, and habits—in short, a cohesive intraclass association, including intermarriage between members of the same class.

Finally, the third and highest level of class is referred to by Marx as that of class-for-itself (*Klasse-für-sich*). This means that a *Klasse-an-sich* that has become a social class has attained full consciousness of its interests and goals and engages in common political activity in pursuit of its class interests.

Thus in capitalist society, the dominant capitalist class, through its control of the major superstructural institutions, obtains political control and disseminates ruling-class ideology, hence assuring its ideological hegemony in society.

At the same time, to prevent the development of class consciousness among the masses and to neutralize and divert their frustration and anger against the system, the dominant class facilitates the development of false consciousness among the working class. This, in turn, serves to block the development of class consciousness among workers and thus prevents, to the extent it is successful, the potential for social revolution.

Nevertheless, the material conditions of life under capitalism eventually incite workers to organize and rise up. As the working class becomes class conscious and discovers that its social condition is the result of its exploitation by the capitalists, it invariably begins to organize and fight back to secure for itself economic benefits and political rights denied in capitalist society—a society wherein the exploitation of labor through the extraction of surplus value is legally assured by the capitalist state.

This exploitation, hence domination, of the working class by capital, Marx points out, would, sooner or later, lead to class struggle, that is, a struggle for political power: "The conflict between proletariat and bourgeoisie is a struggle of one class against another, a struggle that means in its highest expression a total revolution."[11] "Is there any reason to be surprised," Marx asks, "that a society based on class conflict leads to brutal opposition, and in the last resort to a clash between individuals?"[12] "An oppressed class," he maintained, "is the condition of existence of every society based on class conflict. Thus the liberation of the oppressed class necessarily involves the creation of a new society," adding "only in an order of things in which there are no class conflicts will social evolutions cease to be political revolutions."[13]

CLASS STRUGGLE AND THE STATE

Political power, Marx and Engels point out, grows out of economic (class) power driven by money and wealth, but to maintain and secure their wealth, dominant classes of society establish and control political institutions to hold down the masses and to assure their continued domination. The supreme superstructural institution that historically has emerged to carry out this task is the state.

The emergence of the state coincided with the emergence of social classes and class struggles resulting from the transition from a primitive communal to more advanced modes of production when an economic surplus was first generated. Ensuing struggles over control of this surplus led to the development of the state; once captured by the dominant classes in society, the state became an instrument of force to maintain the rule of wealth and privilege against the laboring masses, to maintain exploitation and domination by the few over the many. Without such a powerful instrument of force, there could be no assurance of protection of the privileges of a ruling class, who clearly lived off the labor of the masses. The newly wealthy needed a mechanism that

would not only safeguard the newly-acquired property of private individuals against the communistic traditions of the gentile order, would not only sanctify private property, formerly held in such light esteem, and pronounce this sanctification the highest purpose of human society, but would also stamp the gradually developing new forms of acquiring property, and consequently, of constantly accelerating increase in wealth, with the seal of general public recognition; an institution that would perpetuate, not only the newly-rising class division of society, but also the right of the possessing class to exploit the non-possessing classes and the rule of the former over the latter.

And this institution arrived. The *state* was invented.[14]

Thus the state developed as an institution as a result of the growth of wealth and social classes:

Former society, moving in class antagonisms, had need of the state, that is, an organization of the exploiting class at each period for the maintenance of its external conditions of production; that is, therefore, for the forcible holding down of the exploited class in the conditions of oppression (slavery, villeinage or serfdom, wage labor) determined by the existing mode of production. The state was the official representative of society as a whole, its embodiment in a visible corporation; but it was this only in so far as it was the state of that class which itself, in its epoch, represented society as a whole; in ancient times, the state of the slave-owning citizens; in the Middle Ages, of the feudal nobility; in our epoch, of the bourgeoisie.[15]

In *The Origin of the Family, Private Property and the State*, Engels writes:

It is, as a rule, the state of the most powerful, economically dominant class, which, through the medium of the state, becomes also the politically dominant class, and thus acquires new means of holding down and exploiting the oppressed class. Thus, the state of antiquity was above all the state of the slave owners for the purpose of holding down the slaves, as the feudal state was the organ of the nobility for holding down the peasant serfs and bondsmen, and the modern representative state is an instrument of exploitation of wage labor by capital.[16]

Thus, in all class-divided societies throughout history, "political power is merely the organized power of one class for oppressing another."[17]

In modern capitalist society, the state, reflecting the interests of the dominant capitalist class, can thus be identified as the *capitalist state*, for as Marx and Engels point out, this state is nothing more than a political organ of the bourgeoisie adopted for the "guarantee of their property and interests."[18] Hence, "the bourgeoisie has . . . conquered for itself, in the modern representative State, exclusive political sway. The executive of the modern State is but a committee for managing the common affairs of the whole bourgeoisie."[19] In this sense, the struggle of the working class against capital takes on both an economic *and* a political content:

The more it [the state] becomes the organ of a particular class, the more it directly enforces the supremacy of that class. The fight of the oppressed class against the ruling class becomes necessarily a political fight, a fight first of all against the political dominance of this class.[20]

Seen in this context, the centrality of the state as an instrument of *class rule* takes on an added importance in the analysis of social class and class struggles, for political power contested by the warring classes takes on its real meaning in securing the rule of the victorious class when that power is ultimately exercised through the instrumentality of the state.

Outlined in its clearest and most concise form in his classic work *The State and Revolution*, Lenin explains that in all class societies, the *class essence* of the state's rule over society is rooted in domination and exploitation by a propertied ruling class of the propertyless, oppressed class. In our epoch, writes Lenin, "every state in which private ownership of the land and means of production exists, in which capital dominates, however democratic it may be, is a capitalist state, a machine used by the capitalists to keep the working class and the poor peasants in subjection."[21] Democracy in capitalist society, Lenin points out, "is always bound by the narrow framework of capitalist exploitation, and consequently always remains, in effect, a democracy for the minority, only for the propertied classes, only for the rich."[22]

Freedom in capitalist society always remains about the same as it was in the ancient Greek republics: freedom for the slave-owners. . . .

Democracy for an insignificant minority, democracy for the rich—that is the democracy of capitalist society. . . .

Marx grasped this *essence* of capitalist democracy splendidly when, in analyzing the experience of the Commune, he said that the oppressed are allowed once every few years to decide which particular representatives of the oppressing class shall represent and repress them in parliament![23]

"People always have been the foolish victims of deception and self-deception in politics," Lenin continues elsewhere, "and they always will be until they have learnt to seek out the *interests* of some class or other behind all moral, religious, political and social phrases, declarations and promises."[24]

In class society, Lenin points out, the state has always been "an organ or instrument of violence exercised by one class against another."[25] And in capitalist society, this violence is exercised by the capitalist class against the working class. In an important passage in *The State and Revolution*, Lenin stresses that the state in capitalist society is not only the political organ of the capitalist class; it is structured in such a way that it guarantees the class rule of the capitalists and, short of a revolutionary rupture, its entrenched power is practically unshakable:

A democratic republic is the best possible political shell for capitalism, and, therefore, once capital has gained possession of this very best shell . . . it establishes its power so securely, so firmly, that *no* change of persons, institutions or parties in the bourgeois-democratic republic can shake it.[26]

The question remains: With the obvious contradictions and conflicts between labor and capital, and with the ever-more visible unity of capital and the state, how is it that capital is able to convince broad segments of the laboring masses of the legitimacy of its class rule and the rule of the capitalist state over society?

IDEOLOGICAL HEGEMONY

In explaining the process by which the capitalist class disseminates its ideology through control of the state and its dominance over society, Antonio Gramsci, a prominent Marxist of the early twentieth century, drew attention to the ideological apparatuses of the capitalist state and introduced the concept of bourgeois cultural and ideological *hegemony*.[27] He stressed that it is not enough for the capitalist class simply to take control of the state machine and rule society directly through force and coercion; it must also convince the oppressed classes of the legitimacy of its rule: "The state is the entire complex of practical and theoretical activities with which the ruling class not only justifies and maintains its dominance, but manages to win the active consent of those over whom it rules."[28] Through its dominance of the superstructural organs of the state, the ruling class controls and shapes the ideas, hence consciousness, of the masses. Thus:

Hegemony involves the successful attempts of the dominant class to use its political, moral, and intellectual leadership to establish its view of the world as all-inclusive and universal, and to shape the interests and needs of subordinate groups.[29]

With the acceptance of its ideas and the legitimization of its rule, the capitalist class is able to exercise control and domination of society through its ideological hegemony at the level of the superstructure with the aid and instrumentality of the state. Gramsci, writes Martin Carnoy, "assigned to the State part of this function of promoting a single (bourgeois) concept of reality, and, therefore, gave the State a more extensive (enlarged) role in perpetuating class,"[30] hence preventing the development of working-class consciousness. As such,

It was not merely lack of understanding of their position in the economic process that kept workers from comprehending their class role, nor was it only the "private" institutions of society, such as religion, that were responsible for keeping the working class from self-realization, but it was the *State itself* that was involved in reproducing the relations of production. In other words, the State was much more than the coercive apparatus of the bourgeoisie; the State included the hegemony of the bourgeoisie in the superstructure.[31]

Although the dialectics of the accumulation process, which involves first and foremost the exploitation of labor, ultimately results in class struggle, civil war, and revolution to seize state power, the *ideological hegemony* of the ruling class, operating through the state itself, prolongs bourgeois class rule and institutionalizes and legitimizes exploitation. Gramsci argued that "the system's real strength does not lie in the violence of the ruling class or the coercive power of its state apparatus, but in the acceptance by the ruled of a 'conception of the world' which belongs to the rulers."[32] "False consciousness"—or lack of working-class consciousness and adoption of bourgeois ideas by the laboring masses—Gramsci argued, was the result of a complex process of bourgeois ideological hegemony that, operating through the superstructural (i.e., cultural, ideological, religious, and political) institutions of capitalist society, above all the bourgeois state, came to obtain the consent of the masses in convincing them of the correctness and superiority of the bourgeois worldview.

In his doctrine of "hegemony," Gramsci saw that the dominant class did not have to rely solely on the coercive power of the State or even its direct economic power to rule; rather, through its hegemony, expressed in the civil society *and* the State, the ruled could be persuaded to accept the system of beliefs of the ruling class and to share its social, cultural, and moral values.[33]

"The philosophy of the ruling class," writes Giuseppe Fiori, "passes through a whole tissue of complex vulgarizations to emerge as 'common sense': that is, the philosophy of the masses, who accept the morality, the customs, the institutionalized behavior of the society they live in."[34] "The problem for Gramsci then," Fiori continues, "is to understand *how* the ruling class has managed to win the consent of the subordinate classes in this way; and then, to see how the latter will manage to overthrow the old order and bring about a new one of universal freedom."[35]

The increasing awareness of the working class of this process, hence the development of working-class consciousness, stresses Gramsci, helps expand the emerging class struggle from the economic and social spheres into the sphere of politics and ideology, so the struggle against capitalist ideology promoted by the bourgeois state and other ruling-class institutions becomes just as important, perhaps more so, as the struggle against capital develops and matures in other spheres of society. Countering the ideological hegemony of the capitalist class through the active participation of workers in their own collective organizations, the class-conscious organs of workers' power—militant trade unions, workers' political parties, and so forth—come to play a decisive role in gaining the political support of the laboring masses. In turn, through their newly gained awareness of their own class interests, the workers transcend the bounds of bourgeois ideological hegemony and develop their own counter (proletarian) political outlook—a process that accelerates with the further development of proletarian class consciousness. Thus, as the struggle against the state becomes an important part of the class struggle in general, the struggle against capitalism takes on a truly *political* and *ideological* content.

In the late 1960s, Louis Althusser reintroduced into Marxist discourse Lenin's and Gramsci's contributions on ideology and the state and provided an extended discussion on the basic concepts of historical materialism. Althusser played a key role in the effort to revitalize critical thought on the subject by incorporating the Gramscian notion of ideological hegemony into his own analysis of the "ideological state apparatuses."[36]

In linking the political superstructure to the social-economic base, or mode of production, Althusser argued in favor of the classical Marxist position, which identifies the superstructure as determined "in the last instance" by the base: "The upper floors," he wrote, in reference to the political superstructure, "could not 'stay up' (in the air) alone, if they did not rest precisely on their base."[37] Thus, the state, the supreme political institution and repressive apparatus of society, "enables the ruling classes to ensure their domination over the working class, thus enabling the former to subject the latter to the process of surplus-value extortion."[38] This is so precisely because the state is controlled by the ruling class. And such control makes the state, and the superstructure in general, dependent on and determined by the dominant class in society.

In his essay "Ideology and Ideological State Apparatuses," Althusser expands his analysis of the base-superstructure relationship to include other superstructural institutions—cultural, religious, educational, legal, and so on. As the hegemony of the ruling class in these spheres becomes critical for its control over the dominated classes, and society in general, the class struggle takes on a three-tiered attribute, consisting of the economic, political, and ideological levels. Central to the process of ruling-class ideological domination is the installation by the ruling class of the dominant ideology in the ideological state apparatuses, according to Althusser.

The ideology of the ruling class does not become the ruling ideology by virtue of the seizure of state power alone. It is by the installation of the ideological state apparatuses in which this ideology is realized itself that it becomes the ruling ideology.[39]

The relationship between ruling-class domination and the dominant ideology is also emphasized by Nicos Poulantzas, who further developed Althusser's conceptualization of ideology, situating it in the context of class domination and class struggle. "The dominant ideology, by assuring the practical insertion of agents in the social structure," Poulantzas points out, "aims at the maintenance (the cohesion) of the structure, and this means *above all* class domination and exploitation."[40]

It is precisely in this way that within a social formation ideology is dominated by the ensemble of representations, values, notions, beliefs, etc. by means of which class domination is perpetuated: in other words it is dominated by what can be called the ideology of the dominant class.[41]

This Althusserian conception of the relationship between the base and the superstructure, especially the state and the ideological state apparatuses, came to inform Poulantzas's analysis of classes, class struggle, and the state, and set the stage for subsequent discussion and debate on the Marxist theory of the state.[42]

Whatever their differences in focus of analysis, the contributions of Gramsci, Althusser, and Poulantzas to the Marxist theory of class struggle, the state, and bourgeois ideological hegemony affirm *and* extend the analyses of the Marxist classics and thus advance our understanding of the processes of ruling class domination and hegemony and the responses needed for the transformation of capitalist society.

THE STATE AND REVOLUTION

Writing on the eve of the October Revolution in Russia, Lenin, in his pioneering work *The State and Revolution*, pointed out both the class nature of the state *and*, more important, the necessity of its revolutionary overthrow:

If the state is the product of the irreconcilability of class antagonisms, if it is a power standing *above* society and *"alienating* itself *more and more* from it," it is clear that the liberation of the oppressed class is impossible not only without a violent revolution, *but also without the destruction* of the apparatus of state power which was created by the ruling class and which is the embodiment of this "alienation."[43]

Thus, for Lenin the transformation of capitalist society involves a revolutionary process in which a class-conscious working class, led by a disciplined workers' party, comes to adopt a radical solution to its continued exploitation and oppression under the yoke of capital and exerts its organized political force in a revolutionary rupture to take state power.

The victory of the working class in this struggle for power and control over society leads to establishing a socialist, workers' state. As the class essence of the state lies at the heart of an analysis of the nature and role of the state in different epochs throughout history, the class nature of the socialist state gives us clues to the nature and role of the state in a socialist society developing toward communism. For, as Marx has pointed out in *Critique of the Gotha Program*, the dictatorship of the proletariat (i.e., the class rule of the working class) is a transitional phase between capitalism and communism:

Between capitalist and communist society lies the period of the revolutionary transformation of the one into the other. Corresponding to this is also a political transition period in which the state can be nothing but *the revolutionary dictatorship of the proletariat*.[44]

The class character of the new state under the dictatorship of the proletariat takes on a new content:

Simultaneously with an immense expansion of democracy, which *for the first time* becomes democracy for the poor, democracy for the people, and not democracy for the money-bags, the dictatorship of the proletariat imposes a series of restrictions on the freedom of the oppressors, the exploiters, the capitalists.[45]

Thus, for Lenin the period of transition to communist society exhibits an infinitely higher form of democracy than that found in capitalist society, for democracy under socialism, he argued, is democracy for the masses, democracy for the great majority of the laboring population working together to build an egalitarian, classless society.

CONCLUSION

We have shown that for Marxist theory the concepts of social class and class struggle are central to the analysis of society and social relations. Moreover, Marxism stresses the importance of understanding the dynamics of social change and social transformation within the world historical process. In this context, the understanding of the motive force of historical progress and societal change has brought to the fore the question of political power and the state. In line with its focus on production relations defining the concepts of social class, exploitation, and class struggle as the foundation of the historical materialist approach to the study of society and social life, the centerpiece of Marxist theory has been its focus on the relationship between class structure, class struggles, and the class nature of the state. Situated within the framework of the base-superstructure problematic of historical materialism, the theorists discussed in the preceding pages have been among the pioneers of the Marxist approach to social class and class inequality; other, more recent proponents of historical materialism are playing a central role in further developing the Marxist approach in this final decade of the twentieth century.

NOTES

1. Karl Marx and Frederick Engels, *The German Ideology* (New York: International Publishers, 1947), p. 16.

2. Ibid., p. 7.

3. Frederick Engels, "Letter to Heinz Starkenburg" in K. Marx and F. Engels, *Selected Correspondence* (New York: International Publishers, 1935), p. 516.

4. See Marx and Engels, *The German Ideology*; Karl Marx, *The Poverty of Philosophy* (New York: International Publishers, 1963); Marx, "Preface to *A Contribution to a Critique of Political Economy* in K. Marx and F. Engels, *Selected Works* (New York: International Publishers, 1972); Karl Marx, *Capital*, Vol. 3 (Moscow: Foreign Languages Publishing House, 1962); Frederick Engels, *Anti-Duhring* (New York: International Publishers, 1976), part 2.

5. Karl Marx, "Preface to *A Contribution to the Critique of Political Economy*," p. 182.

6. Marx, *Capital*, Vol. 3, p. 772.

7. Karl Marx and Frederick Engels, "Manifesto of the Communist Party," in Marx and Engels, *Selected Works*, 1972, p. 35.

8. Ibid.

9. Surplus value (or gross profits) is that part of the total value created by labor which workers surrender to the owners of the means of production after receiving only a small portion of the total value in the form of wages. Although the end result is the same, the extraction of surplus value from the producers takes on different forms in social formations dominated by different, historically specific mode(s) of production.

10. Marx and Engels, "Manifesto," p. 36.

11. Marx quoted in Ralph Dahrendorf, *Class and Class Conflict in Industrial Society* (Stanford: Stanford University Press, 1959), p. 18.

12. Ibid.

13. Ibid.

14. Frederick Engels, "The Origin of the Family, Private Property and the State" in Marx and Engels, *Selected Works* (New York: International Publishers, 1972), p. 537.

15. Engels, *Anti-Duhring*, p. 306.

16. Engels, "The Origin," pp. 587–88.

17. Marx and Engels, "Manifesto," p. 53.

18. Marx and Engels, *The German Ideology*, p. 59.

19. Marx and Engels, "Manifesto," p. 37.

20. Frederick Engels, "Ludwig Feuerbach and the End of Classical German Philosophy," in Marx and Engels, *Selected Works*, p. 627.

21. V. I. Lenin, *The State*, in Karl Marx, Frederick Engels, and V. I. Lenin, *On Historical Materialism* (New York: International Publishers, 1974), p. 641.

22. V. I. Lenin, *The State and Revolution*, in V. I. Lenin, *Selected Works in One Volume* (New York: International Publishers, 1971), p. 326.

23. Ibid., pp. 326–27.

24. V. I. Lenin, "The Three Sources and Three Component Parts of Marxism," in Lenin, *Selected Works in One Volume*, p. 24.

25. V. I. Lenin, *Selected Works in Three Volumes*, vol. 2 (Moscow: Progress Publishers, 1975), p. 374.

26. Ibid., p. 272.

27. By *hegemony*, Gramsci meant the ideological predominance of the dominant ruling class(es) over the subordinate. At the same time, and in response to this, he introduced the concept of counterhegemony, which occurs when the proletariat, with the aid of "organic" intellectuals, exerts hegemony and exercises its superiority over society through the establishment of a proletarian socialist state.

28. Antonio Gramsci, *Prison Notebooks* (New York: International Publishers, 1971), p. 244.

29. Martin Carnoy, *The State and Political Theory* (Princeton: Princeton University Press, 1984), p. 70.

30. Ibid., p. 66.

31. Ibid.; emphasis in the original.

32. Giuseppe Fiori, *Antonio Gramsci, Life of a Revolutionary* (London: New Left Books, 1970), p. 238.

33. Carnoy, *The State and Political Theory*, p. 87.

34. Fiori, *Antonio Gramsci*, p. 238.

35. Ibid.

36. See Louis Althusser, *For Marx* (London: Penguin, 1969); idem, *Lenin and Philosophy and Other Essays* (London: New Left Books, 1971). See also Louis Althusser and Etienne Balibar, *Reading Capital* (London: New Left Books, 1968).

37. Althusser, *Lenin and Philosophy and Other Essays*, p. 135.

38. Ibid., p. 137.

39. Ibid., p. 185.

40. Nicos Poulantzas, *Political Power and Social Classes* (London: New Left Books, 1974), p. 209.

41. Ibid.

42. The debate began in the late 1960s with a review of Ralph Miliband's *The State in Capitalist Society* (New York: Basic Books, 1969) by Nicos Poulantzas, "The Problem of the Capitalist State," *New Left Review*, no. 58 (1969), to which Miliband responded in the next issue of the same journal. See Ralph Miliband, "The Capitalist State—Reply to Nicos Poulantzas," *New Left Review*, no. 59 (1970). See also Nicos Poulantzas, *Political Power and Social Classes*; Ralph Miliband, "Poulantzas and the Capitalist State," *New Left Review*, no. 82 (1973); and Nicos Poulantzas, "The Capitalist State: A Reply to Miliband and Laclau," *New Left Review*, no. 95 (1976). Among Poulantzas's later works, see *Classes in Contemporary Capitalism* (London: New Left Books, 1975), and *State, Power, Socialism* (London: New Left Books, 1978). Miliband's subsequent arguments are found in his "Political Forms and Historical Materialism," in R. Miliband and J. Saville (eds.), *Socialist Register, 1975* (London: Merlin Press, 1975); and *Marxism and Politics* (London: Oxford University Press, 1977). See also David Gold, Clarence Y. H. Lo, and Erik Olin Wright, "Some Recent Developments in Marxist Theories of the Capitalist State," parts 1 and 2, *Monthly Review* 27 (October and November 1975); Gosta Esping-Andersen, Roger Friedland, and Erik Olin Wright, "Modes of Class Struggle and the Capitalist State," *Kapitalistate*, nos. 4–5 (Summer 1976); Albert Szymanski, *The Capitalist State and the*

Politics of Class (Cambridge, Mass.: Winthrop, 1978); Bob Jessop, *The Capitalist State* (New York: New York University Press, 1982); Martin Carnoy, *The State and Political Theory.*

43. Lenin, *The State and Revolution*, in V. I. Lenin, *Selected Works* (New York: International Publishers, 1971), p. 268.

44. Karl Marx, *Critique of the Gotha Programme*, in Karl Marx and Frederick Engels, *Selected Works* (New York: International Publishers, 1972), p. 331; emphasis in the original. For an extended discussion on the concept of the "dictatorship of the proletariat," see Etienne Balibar, *On the Dictatorship of the Proletariat* (London: New Left Books, 1977).

45. Lenin, *The State and Revolution*, p. 327; emphasis in original.

Three

The Historical Development of Class Systems

For thousands of years after the formation of human societies, there were no class divisions, hence no class rule over an entire people. In fact, the first known class societies did not arise until about the fourth millennium B.C. Class divisions in society have thus been around for only six thousand years, a relatively short time considering the entire history of human societies. Moreover, most societies during this period were classless. The prevalence of class divisions among a large number of societies around the world became a fact only during the past several hundred years.

THE ORIGINS OF CLASS SOCIETY

Social classes and class struggles emerged during the transition from primitive communal to more advanced modes of production when an economic surplus (i.e., a surplus beyond all that is necessary to feed and clothe a people at the subsistence level) was first generated. In time, struggles between individuals over control of this surplus led to the formation of social classes and resulted in class struggles. These struggles eventually gave rise to the state which, once captured by the dominant classes in society, became an instrument of force to maintain exploitation and domination of the masses.[1]

To trace the historical origins and development of class society, we must go back to the time when human social organization took the form of distinct societies. The first social organization was the commune. Under this mode of social relations, and it accounts for some 80 percent of human history, no classes existed. In primitive hunting and gathering societies with communal social relations, political decisions were made on a collective basis; through tribal councils, all members took part in the decision-making process. Organized along kinship lines, primitive communal societies had no powerful chiefs or strong leaders. In the absence of an institution such as the state, no official authority structure could govern society through force. Instead, voluntary consent to assemblies of the whole tribe constituted the basis of social cooperation to maintain order and effect change. In the absence of class distinctions and private ownership of land, the wealth of society belonged to the whole tribe, and the protection of the tribe's possessions was considered the duty of all its members. In this sense, tribal property, held in common, assured the politics of the primitive commune without the need for a state.

Until about 10,000 years ago, all human societies were at the stage of primitive communism. In fact, until a few hundred years ago, most societies on earth were still of this type. Today, primitive hunting and gathering tribes are found only in a few remote areas of the world. But with the dissolution of the commune between the eighth and fourth millennium B.C.; clan and tribal relations gradually began to change, largely as a result of the growing division of labor among communes and tribes. First, cattle-breeding communes and tribes split off; later, artisans followed suit. Labor productivity began to grow and gave rise to a surplus. The production of food and other necessities surpassed that required for subsistence, and the possibility of accumulation arose. With an increased and formalized division of labor came a rise in inequality and an inequitable distribution of the surplus among clan members. As a result, political power began to be expressed, not in the interests of all members of the clan, but to enrich the chiefs and elders. It also began to be more profitable to make slaves out of prisoners of war than to kill them because they could produce more than they consumed and thus add to the wealth of their owners.

In this way, a minority which amassed wealth was formed in the commune. Organs of self-government began to be changed into organs for the suppression of the majority by the minority. But custom, the moral authority enjoyed by chiefs and joint decision-making were not sufficient any more to turn these organs into regular organs of power. Special detachments (armies, first and foremost) were created to effect, by force of arms, or by the threat of using them, the will of the rich—those who owned the land, livestock and slaves. The appearance of organs of suppression and coercion ushered in the history of the state.[2]

Thus the state developed as a social institution as a result of the growth of wealth and social classes. And the earliest form of society emerging out of the primitive commune where the state assumed a prominent role in societal affairs was Oriental despotism.

ORIENTAL DESPOTIC SOCIETY

With the growth of accumulation and the subsequent disintegration of the tribal communal structure, the state emerged as the supreme political institution in society. It first developed in large river valleys, such as along the Nile, Tigris, Euphrates, Ganges, Yellow, and Yangtze rivers, where despotic empires were set up under the auspices of an imperial court. The consolidation of absolute power by the bureaucratic ruling class and the creation of the great empires of antiquity marked the beginning stage of the history of class society.[3] Over time, highly centralized states began to develop, with large numbers of full-time officials to collect taxes, keep official records, supervise the waterworks, and maintain the police and armies for enforcing the law.

Side by side with the masses thus occupied with one and the same work, we find the "chief inhabitant," who is judge, police, and tax-gatherer in one; the bookkeeper, who keeps the accounts of the village and registers everything relating thereto; another official, who prosecutes criminals, protects strangers travelling through and escorts them to the next village; the boundary man, who guards the boundaries against neighboring communities; the water-overseer, who distributes the water from the common tanks for irrigation [etc.]. . . . This dozen of individuals is maintained at the expense of the whole community.[4]

Moreover, in these societies, the ruler or the emperor had absolute power. All the major institutions—economic, religious, military, and political—were merged into one, centered in an absolute ruler.

The despot here appears as the father of all numerous lesser communities, thus realizing the common unity of all. It, therefore, follows that the surplus product (which, incidentally, is legally determined in terms of [infolge] the real appropriation through labour) belongs to this highest unity. Oriental despotism therefore appears to lead to a legal absence of property. In fact, however, its foundation is tribal or common property, in most cases created through a combination of manufacture and agriculture within the small community which thus becomes entirely self-sustaining and contains within itself all conditions of production and surplus production.

Part of its surplus labor belongs to the higher community, which ultimately appears as a *person*. This surplus labor is rendered both as tribute and as common labor for the glory of the unity, in part that of the despot, in part that of the imagined tribal entity of the god.[5]

The main contradictions in these early class societies, then, were between the masses of people who lived in village units and the ruling class, consisting of the ruler and the state bureaucracy.

An important characteristic of Oriental despotic societies was their strong resistance to change. The Egyptian, Aztec, Incan, Indian, Chinese, and Ottoman empires were highly stable, lasting for several centuries.

Because of their stable nature, change often had to come from external sources.

This was true, for example, in China and India. The despotic empires in these two regions were penetrated by British and, more generally, European capitalism during the later colonial phase of expansion, which broke down all internal barriers to development along the capitalist path. The contemporary capitalist (as well as the feudal) mode was "introduced" from outside the prevailing system of production. This was also true of the Aztec and Incan empires which underwent a similar process of change with the impact of European mercantile expansion to the Americas and the subsequent penetration of commercial and feudal interests in transforming local economic and sociopolitical structures.

With Ottoman despotism, a combination of external *and* internal developments brought change to this centuries-old social formation. Although the expansion of European mercantile capital to the East undermined the Ottoman monopoly on trade in the Mediterranean, an equally important internal process was at work. This was the allocation of parcels of land in rural areas to warriors engaged in the despotic bureaucracy's militaristic adventures in Europe, the Middle East, northern Africa, and elsewhere. This system of land allocation (*timar*) and the subsequent introduction of tax farming (*iltizam*) brought about a major transformation of the Ottoman agrarian structure.[6] The accumulation of large tracts of land, initially by these warriors and later by an emerging landed gentry (*ayan*), led to the development of a landowning class that came to subordinate local communal villagers to its dictates. Through this process, the majority of the local population was turned into an unpaid laboring class tied to local landed interests and in a position not unlike the serfs under European feudalism. At the same time, interaction with Europe facilitated the expansion of European commercial capital into the empire and led to the transformation of the local merchant class into an intermediary of European capital. In this way, the state came to represent the interests of the landed gentry, local merchants, and European capital, as well as the political bureaucracy on which it was based.[7]

In other despotic societies, an alternative path of development led to the emergence of slavery and feudalism as dominant modes of production. The transition from Oriental despotic state under the Asiatic mode of production to its varied forms under slavery and feudal landlordism was a process that took hundreds of years. But, in time, the development of new modes of production resulted in transforming the superstructure as well, in a way that directly corresponded to the prevailing relations of production and the ensuing class struggles. Thus the evolution of changing property relations in society ushered in a new form of the state—a state that served the interests of new ruling classes (of slave owners, landlords, and subsequently, capitalists) for purposes of control, domination, and exploitation of the laboring masses.

ANCIENT SLAVE-OWNING SOCIETY

In some societies, the state possessed immense power and served to advance the interests of masters against slaves. Societies based on the slave mode of production, such as Athens, were located along major trade routes and at the mouths of important rivers. They became major trading centers with strong military power.

In the ancient world commerce and the development of commercial capital . . . resulted in a slave economy, or sometimes, depending on the point of departure, it resulted simply in the transformation of a patriarchal slave system devoted to the production of direct means of subsistence into a similar system devoted to the production of surplus value.[8]

In ancient society, then, the dominant mode of production was slavery, and the surplus extracted from slaves was appropriated by the citizen ruling class, or masters.

Slave-owning societies conquered large numbers of people and made them slaves. This practice enabled Athens to maintain a democracy for Athenian citizens while enslaving virtually all the people in the surrounding environs: "In Athens," writes V. Gordon Childe, "democracy was made completely effective. . . . Every citizen was expected to attend assemblies and to sit on juries. . . . In the latter part of the fifth century, countrymen did in fact attend the assembly and vote on questions of general policy."[9]

Fifth-century Athens thus provides the first adequately documented example of a through-going popular government. Its popular character must not be exaggerated. In the first place women had no place in public life. . . . Secondly, citizenship was now a hereditary privilege from which resident aliens were rigorously excluded. . . . Finally, industry was based on slavery; even the small farmer generally owned a slave or two, and the majority of the employees in mines and factories . . . were slaves. . . . [A]liens had no share in the government and slaves had no rights whatever.[10]

The primary contradiction in the productive scheme of ancient societies, such as Athens and early Rome, was between slaves and masters. While the surplus product created by forced (slave) labor was converted into unproductive expenditure—on public works, religious monuments, and works of art, as well as the extravagant, aristocratic way of life of the citizen ruling class—the condition of the slave masses deteriorated, and their position of subsistence became more precarious as their impoverishment grew.[11]

The decay of ancient social organization was the result of a decline in trade, the money economy, and cities, all of which—accompanied by war, expansion, and a constant increase in slavery and, with it, widespread slave rebellions[12]—made slavery no longer profitable and undermined the entire community structure. These developments led to the slaves' conversion into proto-serfs, that is, neither citizens nor slaves. Although this meant a certain level of improvement in their position compared to earlier periods, they nonetheless remained tied to the land and were bought and sold with it. Herein lay the preconditions for the transition to feudalism.

FEUDAL SOCIETY

The origins of classical European feudalism go back to the Germanic invasions of the Roman Empire and the fusion of the essentially household-based Germanic mode with Roman proto-feudalism, which occurred after the collapse of the slave system of ancient Rome. The forced unity of the two societies, originally at different stages of development, led to the eventual dissolution of the old forms and gave rise to the development of a yet new (feudal) mode of production.

The last centuries of the declining Roman Empire and its conquest by the barbarians destroyed a number of productive forces; agriculture had declined, industry had decayed for lack of markets, trade had died out or had been violently interrupted, and the rural and urban population had diminished. These conditions and the mode of organization of the conquest determined by them gave rise, under the influence of the Teutonic military constitution, to feudal property.[13]

The essential social relation of production in feudal societies was between lord and serf. There was very little division of labor, minimal trade or commerce (as all goods were produced in self-sufficient communities), and constant warfare among feudal lords to expand land. The village was the basic unit of the agrarian feudal economy and consisted of a population ranging from about a dozen to several hundred peasant families living in a cluster. The manor, in contrast, was a unit of political jurisdiction and economic exploitation controlled by a single lord; it was often geographically identical with the village, although some manors embraced two or more villages.

The village community [was] a closed system, economically self-sufficient, capable of sustaining the material and spiritual needs of the villages without much contact with the outside world.... The economy of the Early Middle Ages, lacking a vigorous commercial life and a significant urban population, failed to provide villages with much incentive to produce beyond their immediate needs. There was only the most limited market for surplus grain. Accordingly, village life tended to be uneventful, tradition-bound, and circumscribed by the narrowest of horizons....

Superimposed on the economic structure of the village was the political-juridical structure of the manor. The average peasant was bound to a manorial lord.... They owed various dues to their manorial lord, chiefly in kind, and were normally expected to labor for a certain number of days per week—often three—on the lord's fields.[14]

The obligations placed on the peasants were immense, and their function within the manorial system was one of productive subordination to the lord. In addition to their obligation to work on the lord's fields, the peasants paid their lord a percentage of the produce of their fields, as well as paying various fees and taxes. The following key excerpt from Engels's *The Peasant War in Germany* captures the condition of life of the peasant in feudal Germany:

At the bottom of all the classes, save the last one, was the huge exploited mass of the nation, the peasants. It was the peasant who carried the burden of all the other strata of society: princes, officialdom, nobility, clergy, patricians and middle-class. Whether the peasant was the subject of a prince, an imperial baron, a bishop, a monastery, or a city, he was everywhere treated as a beast of burden and worse. If he was a serf, he was entirely at the mercy of his master.... Most of his time, he had to work on his master's estate. Out of that which he earned in his few free hours, he had to pay tithes, dues, ground rents, war taxes, land taxes, imperial taxes and other payments. He could neither marry nor die without paying the master.... The community meadows and woods of the peasants had almost everywhere been forcibly taken away by the masters.[15]

Engels points out that the domination of the lord or master over the peasant extended not only over the peasant's property but also over his person:

And in the same manner as the master reigned over the peasant's property, he extended his wilfulness over his person, his wife and daughters. He possessed the right of the first night. Whenever he pleased, he threw the peasant into the tower, ... killed him or ordered him beheaded. None of the instructive chapters of the Carolina[16] which speaks of "cutting of ears," "cutting of noses," "blinding," "chopping of fingers," "beheading," "breaking on the wheel," "burning," "pinching with burned tongs," "quartering," etc., was left unpracticed by the gracious lord and master at his pleasure. Who could defend the peasant? The courts were manned by barons, clergymen, patricians, or jurists, who knew very well for what they were being paid. Not in vain did all the official estates of the empire lie on the exploitation of the peasants.[17]

Although state rule was highly decentralized, and there was little in the way of a state bureaucracy, the power of the feudal lords rested on their military strength: "The hierarchical system of landownership, and the armed bodies of retainers associated with it, gave the nobility power over the serfs. This feudal structure was, just as much as the communal property of antiquity, an association against a subject producing class, but the form of association and the relation to the direct producers were different because of the different conditions of production."[18]

Historically, the feudal mode of production in Western Europe began to give way to mercantilism in the sixteenth century. The growth of trade and the rise of the merchant class strengthened the rule of the state, which obtained monopoly over trade and the economy in general during the mercantile era and set the groundwork for the subsequent emergence of capitalism and the capitalist state.[19]

The transition from feudalism to mercantilism was marked by a transformation of the state from a coordinating institution of dispersed landed interests over a large agrarian territory to a centralized power representing the new merchant class concentrated in urban trading centers and port cities. The shift in the center of political rule thus resulted from a shift in production relations, and relations of exploitation in general, in favor of the merchant class in league with the early capitalists in transition from crafts production to large-scale manufacturing and industry. The protection provided to the merchants by the mercantile state in the transitional period resulted from the increasing power and influence of the merchant class in economic life and consequently in politics. In time, the merchants constituted the new ruling class in Europe (and elsewhere).[20]

The reappearance of a strong central state coincided with the dissolution of the feudal mode of production and the rise to prominence of the merchant class. Through the powers of the state, they ushered in a period of mercantilism. At the height of mercantilism, and with a greatly expanded overseas trade during the sixteenth to eighteenth centuries in Europe, we begin to see the emergence of the original accumulation of capital that subsequently gave rise to capitalism in Western Europe. Thus, overseas trade, the basis of the original accumulation of capital, played a crucial role in weakening the position of the landlords, in laying the foundations of capitalism and thereby facilitating the process of transition.[21]

The discovery of America, the rounding of the Cape, opened up fresh ground for the rising bourgeoisie. The East-Indian and Chinese markets, the colonization of America, trade with the colonies, the increase in the means of exchange and in commodities generally, gave to commerce, to navigation, to industry, an impulse never before known, and thereby, to the revolutionary element in the tottering feudal society, a rapid development.[22]

As trade and merchant's capital set the stage for the shift toward manufacturing and industrial production for further accumulation, the balance of forces in the economy began to swing in favor of the rising bourgeoisie, whose growing wealth and economic strength brought changes in the nature and role of the state as well—in favor of the bourgeoisie.

At the same pace at which the progress of modern industry developed, widened, intensified the class antagonism between capital and labor, the State power assumed more and more the character of the national power of capital over labour, of a public force organized for social enslavement, of an engine of class despotism.[23]

The absolutist monarchies that ruled much of Europe in an earlier period and were strengthened during the mercantilist era through strong state intervention in the economy worked to the benefit of the bourgeoisie as its expanded economic position vis-à-vis the landlords and the merchants, and the subsequent political pressure it exerted upon the state, resulted in the state's increasing isolation from the control and influence of the former ruling classes in both the economy and the polity. In time, the bourgeoisie forced a dissolution of the absolutist state and established republics (in France and Switzerland) or constitutional monarchies (in England and Holland). Eventually, the bourgeoisie set up its own states throughout much of Europe and ushered in a new era of capitalist expansion promoted and safeguarded by the new capitalist state.

CAPITALIST SOCIETY

The decline of feudalism and the rise of capitalism in Europe marked the beginning of a new chapter in world history. The transition from the feudal to the capitalist mode was accompanied by a number of preconditions that gave rise to capitalism and capitalist relations, and came to dominate the social formations of Western Europe by the early eighteenth century.

In examining the decline of feudalism and the rise of capitalism in Western Europe, Marx conceived of two possible paths of development that could lead to the emergence of capitalism in formations previously dominated by the feudal mode: (1) merchant to capitalist, and (2) craftsman to capitalist. Of the two, Marx characterized the second as the "really revolutionary way," pointing to the centrality of the internal contradictions lodged in the productive process under feudalism, which contained the germs of the emergent capitalist mode in the form of petty commodity production based on crafts.[24]

This was clearly true in Britain and France, where the new forces of production came into the hands of small craftsmen, who set up workshops and factories employing wage labor, thus transforming themselves into capitalists. In Prussia and most of Eastern Europe, however, the big merchants and landlords became the owners of industry. In the absence of a strong, independent capitalist class, and with power in the hands of the merchants and landlords, capitalism in this region developed gradually and over an extended time; monarchist and feudal forms of the state continued to dominate society well into the twentieth century.[25]

Marx's careful examination of the European experience convinced him that, on balance, a combination of the two paths, dominated more by the first, actually led to the emergence of capitalism and capitalist relations in much of Europe. This prompted him to emphasize the importance of trade (especially colonial trade) as a major contributing factor in the dissolution of feudalism and the original accumulation of capital. This was the case in addition to the fundamental internal contradictions of the feudal mode, where trade provided the added impetus in bringing about the collapse of feudalism:

Trade with the colonies, the increase in the means of exchange and in commodities generally, gave to commerce, to navigation, to industry, an impulse never before known, and thereby, to the revolutionary element in the tottering feudal society, a rapid development. . . .

In proportion as industry, commerce, navigation, railways extended, in the same proportion the bourgeoisie developed, increased its capital, and pushed into the background every class handed down from the Middle Ages.[26]

Historically, a number of conditions set the stage and led to the emergence of capitalism and the capitalist state in Western Europe and elsewhere. These included the availability of free laborers, the generation of moneyed wealth, a sufficient level of skills and technology, markets, and the protection provided by the state. In general, these conditions were the foundations on which a precapitalist society transformed itself into a capitalist one until capitalism developed through its own dynamics.[27] Once capitalism was established, it began to produce and reproduce the conditions for expanded commodity production and capital accumulation. From this point on, capitalism developed in accordance with its inherent contradictions.

With the principal relations of production that between wage labor and the owners of the means of production, capitalism established itself as a mode of production based on the exploitation of wage labor by capitalists, whose power and authority in society derived from their ownership and control of the means of production. Lacking ownership of the means necessary to gain a living, producers were forced to sell their labor power to capitalists in order to survive. As a result, the surplus value produced by labor was appropriated by the capitalists in the form of profit. Thus, private profit, generated through the exploitation of labor, became the motive force of capitalism.

The contradictions imbedded in such antagonistic social relations in time led to the radicalization of workers and the formation of trade unions and other labor organizations that played important roles in the ensuing class struggles between labor and capital. The history of the labor movement in Europe, the United States, and elsewhere in the world is replete with bloody confrontations between labor and capital and the latter's repressive arm, the capitalist state. From the early battles of workers in Great Britain and on the Continent in the late eighteenth and early nineteenth centuries, to the decisive role played by French workers in the uprising of 1848–1851, to the Paris Commune in 1871, to the Haymarket affair and the heroic struggle of the Knights of Labor and the Industrial Workers of the World in the United States in the late nineteenth and early twentieth centuries, the working class has put up a determined struggle in its fight against capital on both sides of the Atlantic—a struggle spanning over two centuries.

Established to protect and advance the interests of the capitalist class, the early capitalist state assumed a pivotal role that assured the class rule of capitalists over society and thus became an institution of legitimization and brute force to maintain law and order in favor of capitalism. Sanctioning and enforcing laws to protect the rights of the new property owners and disciplining labor to maintain a wage system that generated profits for the wealthy few, the capitalist state became the instrument of capital and its political rule over society.

Among the major functions of the early capitalist states (e.g., in Great Britain and the United States in the nineteenth century) were guaranteeing private property at home and abroad; collecting taxes; recording births, deaths, and income for purposes of taxation and raising armies; guaranteeing contracts; providing the infrastructure (railroads, canals, communication) for the new industries; facilitating the growth of private industry; mediating among various wealthy interests; securing a cheap and disciplined labor force for private enterprise; and preserving law and order to keep the masses under control. Corresponding to conditions under early industrial capitalism, the state had only a small bureaucracy, spent little on social programs, and had a relatively small standing army; taxes were greatly reduced and were collected largely through tariffs on imports in order to protect home industry.[28]

The central task of the early capitalist state in Europe and the United States was that of disciplining the labor force. Union activity, strikes, or collective actions of any kind by workers against businesses were prohibited; demonstrations, agitation, and other forms of struggle initiated by workers against the employers and the system were systematically repressed. Thus, while state intervention in the economy was kept to a minimum to permit the capitalists to enrich themselves without regulation, the capitalist-controlled state became heavily involved in the conflict between labor and capital on behalf of the capitalist class, bringing to bear its repressive apparatus on labor and its allies who threatened the capitalist order. Law and order enforced by the state in early capitalism (and right up to the present) served to protect and preserve the capitalist system and prevent its transformation. In this sense, the state came to see itself as a legitimizing agency of the new social order and identified its survival directly with the capitalists who controlled it. This mutual relationship between state and capital in time set the conditions for the structural environment in which the state promoted capitalist interests, now without the necessity of direct control by individual capitalists through specific state agencies. Within this process of the state's development from early to mature capitalism, the structural imperatives of capital accumulation placed the state in the service of capital, thus transforming it into a capitalist state.

SOCIALIST SOCIETY

Emerging from a revolution against the capitalist system, socialist society is a new type of society ruled by the working class and the laboring masses. The cornerstone of a workers' state, emerging out of capitalism and the remnants of feudalism, is the abolition of private property in the major means of production and an end to the exploitation of labor for private profit. The establishment of a revolutionary democratic society ruled by the working class (as against the rule of capital) is what distinguishes a socialist society from its capitalist counterpart.[29]

In socialist society the state represents and protects the interests of the working class against capital and all other vestiges of reactionary exploitative classes, which, overthrown and dislodged from power, attempt in a multitude of ways to recapture the state through a counterrevolution. "The theory of the class struggle, applied by Marx to the question of the state and the socialist revolution," writes Lenin,

leads as a matter of course to the recognition of the *political rule* of the proletariat. . . . The overthrow of the bourgeoisie can be achieved only by the proletariat becoming the *ruling class*, capable of crushing the inevitable and desperate resistance of the bourgeoisie, and of organizing *all* the working and exploited people for the new economic system.[30]

In this context, then, the proletarian state has a dual role to play: (1) to break the resistance of its class enemies (the exploiting classes), and (2) to protect the revolution and begin the process of socialist construction. The class character of the new state under socialism takes on a new form and content.

During this period the state must inevitably be a state that is democratic *in a new way* (for the proletariat and the propertyless in general) . . . with an immense expansion of democracy, which *for the first time* becomes democracy for the poor, democracy for the people, and not democracy for the money-bags.[31]

Used primarily to build the material base of a classless, egalitarian society, the socialist state begins to wither away once there is no longer any need for its existence:

The first act in which the state really comes forward as the representative of society as a whole—the taking possession of the means of production in the name of society [under socialism]—is at the same time its last independent act as a state. The interference of the state power in social relations becomes superfluous in one sphere after another, and then ceases of itself. The government of persons is replaced by the administration of things and the direction of the processes of production. The state is not "abolished," *it withers away.*[32]

In this sense, the state no longer exists in the fully matured communist stage, for there is no longer the need in a classless society for an institution that is, by definition, an instrument of class rule through force and violence.

Only in communist society, when the resistance of the capitalists has been completely crushed, when the capitalists have disappeared, when there are no classes (i.e., when there is no distinctions between the members of society as regards their relation to the social means of production), *only* then "the state . . . ceases to exist," and *"it becomes possible to speak of freedom."*[33]

It is thus in this broader, transitional context that the class nature and tasks of the state in socialist society must be understood and evaluated.

Historically, the October Revolution in Russia marked the first successful twentieth-century proletarian revolution that brought workers to state power. Thus the new Soviet state soon became the prime example of a revolutionary proletarian socialist state. In the years since 1917, workers and peasants have risen up in many lands to free themselves from feudal-capitalist exploitation. In China, Vietnam, Korea, Cuba, and many other countries, the victorious laboring masses have, through working-class leadership, set out to build a new egalitarian society.

The extent to which today's self-proclaimed socialist states approximate the theoretical formulations of the Marxist classics on the nature of socialist society is hotly debated among the Left. Whether the former Soviet Union, China, Cuba, and other postcapitalist states are to be classified as socialist societies (i.e., ruled by the working class) has often been influenced by political ideology and party affiliation, rather than by a concrete analysis of the nature of these societies.[34]

The recent changes that many East European societies as well as the former Soviet Union have undergone in the early 1990s are now beginning to generate a new set of contradictions that will in time set these societies on a new course of societal transformation that is currently in the making.

CONCLUSION

The history of human social organization and societal transformation through the ages illustrates that class society is a relatively recent phenomenon, and that class divisions in society across time and space have not only varied in accordance with the changing material conditions of life under different modes of production but they are also increasingly being challenged as unnatural and exploitative constructs of human society. Throughout the past several millennia, since the dissolution of the primitive commune, societies around the world have in different ways experienced the domination of one class by another, hence the exploitation and oppression of subordinate classes by those that own and control the means of economic production and social-political repression through the state. But the dialectics of this process of domination has at the same time generated its own contradictions and conflicts, leading to class struggles everywhere. From the slave revolts of ancient times, through the peasant wars of medieval feudalism, to the modern proletarian struggles of advanced capitalism, the subordinate classes of society across the world have risen up *en masse*, challenging the very basis of the prevailing social order.

The conclusions to be drawn from our analysis of different types of societies with their dominant modes of production and corresponding class relations can be summed up by reference to the class struggle as the primary motive force of history. If history is to be viewed as a progression of social development over time, then class struggle must be seen as the engine of that development that propels human social relations to a higher level through the resolution of contradictions that continue to afflict society as we aim at the highest levels of human social existence in the coming twenty-first century.

NOTES

1. Frederick Engels, *The Origin of the Family, Private Property and the State* (New York: International Publishers, 1972), p. 263.

2. Gennady Belov, *What Is the State?* (Moscow: Progress Publishers, 1986), p. 21.

3. On the nature of Oriental despotic society and the Asiatic mode of production, see Perry Anderson, *Lineages of the Absolutist State* (London: New Left Books, 1974), pp. 462–549; Hal Draper, *Karl Marx's Theory of Revolution* (New York: Monthly Review Press, 1977), pp. 515–71; D. R. Gandy, *Marx and History* (Austin and London: University of Texas Press, 1979), pp. 18–25; and Lawrence Krader, *The Asiatic Mode of Production* (Assen: Van Gorcum, 1975).

4. Karl Marx, *Capital, vol. 1 (New York: International Publishers, 1967), pp. 357–58.*

5. Karl Marx, *Pre-Capitalist Economic Formations* (New York: International Publishers, 1965), pp. 69–70.

6. Halil Inalcik, *The Ottoman Empire* (New York: Praeger, 1973); H. Islamoglu and S. Faroqhi, "Crop Patterns and Agricultural Production Trends in Sixteenth-Century Anatolia," *Review* 2, no. 3 (Winter 1979), pp. 401–36.

7. For further discussion on the nature of the Ottoman Empire and the controversy surrounding the applicability of the Asiatic mode of production to the Ottoman social formation, see Sencer Divitcioglu, *Asya Uretim Tarzi ve Osmanli*

Toplumu (The Asiatic Mode of Production and Ottoman Society) (Istanbul: Koz Yayinevi, 1971); Ozlem Ozgur, *Sanayilesme ve Turkiye* (Industrialization and Turkey) (Istanbul: Gercek Yayinevi, 1976), pp. 100–132; and Ismail Cem, *Turkiyede Geri Kalmisligin Tarihi* (The History of Underdevelopment in Turkey) (Istanbul: Cem Yayinevi, 1970), pp. 53–139. For a critical view and an attempted refutation of the Asiatic mode thesis (stressing that Ottoman society was from the beginning a feudal society), see Dogan Avcioglu, *Turkiye'nin Duzeni* (Turkey's Social Order) (Istanbul: Ant Yayinevi, 1975), pp. 13–31.

8. Karl Marx, *Selected Writings in Sociology and Social Philosophy* (New York: McGraw-Hill, 1964), p. 113.

9. V. Gordon Childe, *What Happened in History* (Baltimore: Penguin, 1971), p. 215.

10. Ibid., p. 216.

11. Engels, *Origin*, pp. 217–37.

12. As Childe points out: "slave revolts . . . assumed serious proportions for the first time in history after 134 B.C. Attica, Macedonia, Delos, Sicily, Italy, and Pergamon. The rebels were often joined by small peasants and tenants and even by 'free' proletarians." Childe, *What Happened in History*, p. 267.

13. Marx, *Selected Writings in Sociology*, p. 117–18.

14. C. Warren Hollister, *Medieval Europe*, 3rd ed. (New York: Wiley, 1974), pp. 131–32.

15. Frederick Engels, *The Peasant War in Germany* (New York: International Publishers, 1973), p. 47.

16. *Carolina*, a criminal code of the sixteenth century, published in 1532 under Emperor Charles V.

17. Engels, *The Peasant War in Germany*, pp. 47–48.

18. Marx, *Selected Writings in Sociology*, p. 118.

19. See Immanuel Wallerstein, *The Modern World System* (New York: Academic Press, 1974); idem, *The Capitalist World Economy* (Cambridge: Cambridge University Press, 1979); and idem, *The Politics of the World Economy* (Cambridge: Cambridge University Press, 1984).

20. Wallerstein, *The Modern World System*.

21. For an analysis of the debate on the transition from feudalism to capitalism in Western Europe, see Berch Berberoglu, "The Transition from Feudalism to Capitalism: The Sweezy-Dobb Debate," *Revista Mexicana de Sociologia*, December 1977. The original debate between Sweezy and Dobb, which took place in the pages of the journal *Science and Society* in the early 1950s, is compiled, with additional commentaries and discussion, in *The Transition from Feudalism to Capitalism*, ed. Rodney Hilton (London: New Left Books, 1976).

22. Karl Marx and Frederick Engels, "Manifesto of the Communist Party," in Karl Marx and Frederick Engels, *Selected Works* (New York: International Publishers, 1972), p. 36.

23. Karl Marx, "The Civil War in France," in Marx and Engels, *Selected Works*, p. 289.

24. Karl Marx, *Capital*, vol. 1 (New York: International Publishers, 1967).

25. See Perry Anderson, *Passages from Antiquity to Feudalism* (London: New Left Books, 1974).

26. Karl Marx and Frederick Engels, "Manifesto of the Communist Party," pp. 36–37.

27. Karl Marx, *Pre-Capitalist Economic Formations* (New York: International Publishers, 1965).

28. In other parts of the world (e.g., Germany and Japan), the state took a more active role in production and industrial expansion as it came to manage major sectors of the economy directly. See Barrington Moore, Jr., *The Social Origins of Democracy and Dictatorship* (London: Penguin, 1968); and John Clapham, *The Economic Development of France and Germany* (Cambridge: Cambridge University Press, 1948).

29. Karl Marx, *Critique of the Gotha Programme*, in Karl Marx and Frederick Engels, *Selected Works* (New York: International Publishers, 1972), p. 331.

30. V. I. Lenin, *The State and Revolution*, in V. I. Lenin, *Selected Works in One Volume* (New York: International Publishers, 1971), p. 281.

31. Ibid., pp. 288, 327.

32. F. Engels, *Anti-Duhring* (New York: International Publishers, 1976), p. 307.

33. Lenin, *State and Revolution*, pp. 327–28.

34. A variety of political positions have characterized the Soviet Union in the pre-1991 period as capitalist or socialist across the political spectrum on the left. See, for example, Paul Sweezy and Charles Bettelheim (eds.), *On the Transition to Socialism* (New York: Monthly Review Press, 1971); Charles Bettelheim, *Class Struggles in the USSR*, 2 vols. (New York: Monthly Review Press, 1976 and 1978); Martin Nicolaus, *Restoration of Capitalism in the USSR* (Chicago: Liberator Press, 1975); Revolutionary Union, *How Capitalism Has Been Restored in the Soviet Union* (Chicago: The Revolutionary Union, 1974); Tony Cliff, *State Capitalism in Russia* (London: Pluto Press, 1974); Michael Goldfield and Melvin Rothenberg, *The Myth of Capitalism Reborn: A Marxist Critique of Theories of Capitalist Restoration in the USSR* (San Francisco: Line of March Publications, 1980); Sam Marcy, *The Class Character of the USSR* (New York: World View Publishers, 1977); Erwin Marquit, *The Socialist Countries* (Minneapolis: MEP Press, 1978). Also see Albert Szymanski, *Is the Red Flag Flying? The Political Economy of the Soviet Union* (London: Zed Press, 1979).

Four

Class Structure of Advanced Capitalist Societies

The class structure of advanced capitalist societies is characterized by the two chief contending classes in the production process—labor and capital—that have been engaged in struggle since the emergence of capitalism in Europe and later in the United States and elsewhere in the world. While numerous other classes—such as landowners, family farmers, small independent business owners, and the permanently unemployed—have always existed within the social-economic boundaries of the capitalist system throughout the world, the capitalist class and the working class are the two major antagonistic classes that define the main parameters of class relations and class conflict in capitalist society.

The defining characteristic of the rival classes in advanced capitalist society is the relationship that these classes have to the ownership and control of the means of production. The capitalist class owns and controls the means of production and accumulates capital through the exploitation of labor. Surplus value—the value produced by the workers over and above the wages they receive—is extracted by the capitalists in the form of profits for purposes of accumulation of wealth and capital. The working class, on the other hand, does not own means of production and labors for the capitalist for wages in order to live. This relationship in the production sphere which has a social-economic character becomes a political one as soon as the classes in question struggle to advance their own interests. The class struggle, therefore, is first and foremost a political struggle for gains in the social-economic sphere but ultimately leads to a struggle for state power. The control of the state by the capitalist class makes the state a capitalist state, just as its revolutionary transformation into a workers' state by the working class turns it into a socialist state.

To understand the logic of this process in a concrete fashion, we shall examine below the development of the class structure in the United States—the leading capitalist nation of the late twentieth century. Through such analysis we can come to a better understanding of the material bases of social transformations in capitalist society that are rooted in class relations and class struggles.

THE DEVELOPMENT OF THE CLASS STRUCTURE IN THE UNITED STATES

Over the past two centuries, the United States has developed into an advanced capitalist society and with it has witnessed transformation of its class structure. With the abolition of slavery and the triumph of industrial capitalism in the late nineteenth century, the U.S. class structure came to increasingly reflect the changes in the U.S. economy and society as manifested in the class nature of the state and the balance of class forces in society.

From its inception in 1776 to the end of the Civil War in 1865, the state in the United States represented the interests of both the emerging capitalist class in the North and the planter or slave-owning class in the South, which was tied to the British-dominated world economy. Specializing in agroindustrial raw material production (e.g., cotton) geared to the needs of the textile industry in England, the slave-owning class in the South came to articulate the interests of its ex-colonial master poised against northern capital, from which it carved out for itself a portion of the profits guaranteed by the imperial crown. The contradictory class relationship between the two rival ruling classes in postcolonial America continued to evolve and develop within the framework of a truce that permitted the coexistence of two distinct modes of production through the sharing of state power, at least for a time.

The balance of class forces in the state apparatus from the postindependence period to the Civil War was maintained by the Constitution drawn up by these two rival propertied classes in 1787—a Constitution that would give power to a central state in order to protect the interests of these classes and to prevent popular democratic control of the government. Fifty-three of the fifty-five delegates to the Convention were or represented the economic interests of slave-owners, merchants, creditors, and manufacturers.[1] Forty of the delegates held the paper money issued by the Continental Congress to finance the Revolutionary War, fourteen held vast tracts of land, twenty-four were creditors and mortgage holders, eleven were merchants or manufacturers, and fifteen were slave owners.[2] Moreover, according to James McHenry, a delegate from Maryland, at least twenty-one of the fifty-five delegates favored some form of monarchy.[3] In short, the framers of the Constitution wanted to establish a state guided by principles and laws reflecting the interests of the propertied classes as against those of the slaves, the workers, the artisans, and the farmers, as well as the Native American people, in effect the vast majority of the population.[4] The critical linkage between class and state in postcolonial America, then, was established precisely by the class nature and role of the Constitution which provided the basis of the rule of property over labor and gave the state its subsequent class character.[5] For this reason, the Constitution can be seen both as a product *and* as an instrument of the class forces that came to dominate the U.S. state until the Civil War.

It soon became clear, however, that the state apparatus that came under the control of the ruling classes could not function properly unless some mechanisms of mediation of conflict were instituted to resolve differences between rival forces within the ruling-class coalition. Thus, "in order to regulate the conflict of interests between capitalists and landowners, a series of checks and balances between judiciary, congressional, and executive powers were introduced, as well as different methods of representation for the Senate and the House of Representatives."[6] During the first half of the nineteenth century, slave owners were the dominant force within the ruling-class alliance. This is evidenced by the fact that key positions within the federal machinery were controlled by slave owners, assisted by their financial and mercantile allies in the North. The executive and legislative branches of the state were pro-slave owner, and seven of the nine Supreme Court justices were either slave owners or supported slavery. By the middle of the nineteenth century, capitalist development had reached new heights throughout the North, requiring new markets, access to raw materials, cheap and abundant labor, and further capital accumulation. The slave-owning class in the South held on to its source of wealth through the exploitation of slave labor. The contradictions that had been developing between the two systems since the formation of the Union could no longer be contained within the existing state. Thus the two exploiting classes finally clashed to solve, once and for all, the question of state power.

The level of development reached by the different modes of production at the time of independence was such that it took nearly a century for these contradictions to come to a head and culminate in a civil war that would finally determine the answer to the decisive question: Which class alone shall rule the state? The northern, capitalist victory against the slave-owning South resulted in the transfer of state power to the capitalist class and thereby ushered in the rule of the capitalist state. In this sense, the northern victory in the Civil War marked a turning point in the social transformation of postcolonial America, when capitalism became the dominant mode of production and the capitalist state the dominant political authority in the land.

As capitalism came to dominate the national economy and polity following the Civil War, the primary struggle became that between industrial capital (and its associated moneyed interests) on the one side and the small farmers and a growing class of industrial workers on the other. During this period of "reconstruction" (i.e., the period of transition to and establishment of capitalist dominance), "the capitalist class turned the state completely into its instrument. The state heavily subsidized the building of the railways and internal improvements. High protective tariffs were established. Immigration of laborers was encouraged.... In every way the state facilitated the rapid and unimpeded advance of industrial capital."[7] As a result, a tremendous expansion of capital took place, leading to the concentration and centralization of wealth in the hands of the capitalists, whose base of exploitation expanded through the accumulation of surplus value from both local and immigrant labor. With the growth of industry and the expansion of production, capitalism began to spread throughout the nation. The ex-slaves (now paid wage labor), together with the established industrial proletariat of the northern cities, generated ever-higher rates of surplus value for the capitalists, yielding huge profits and fueling the fortunes of the superrich who set up immense financial empires that generated the first capitalist monopolies, cartels, and trusts. Through this process of expansion, capital, now in its monopoly stage, came to dominate the U.S. economy, state, and society by the late nineteenth and early twentieth centuries. As a result, the state's role in regulating the economy in favor of capital began to grow, as did its role in repressing an increasingly militant working class.

Beginning in the first two decades of this century and continuing throughout the Great Depression and World War II, the state played a key role in safeguarding and promoting the capitalist economy. With its entry into World War II, the United States embarked on the road to full recovery and thereby became a powerful force on the world scene. Within a short period of time at the war's end the United States emerged as the leading imperial power and became the dominant economic, political, and military force in the world. The postwar expansion of U.S. capital on a world scale that the U.S. state came to facilitate during this period in turn resulted in the global expansion of the U.S. state; together these developments came to express in the latter half of the twentieth century the widening interests of U.S. monopoly capital throughout the world.

THE CONTEMPORARY CLASS STRUCTURE OF THE UNITED STATES

The unprecedented expansion of the U.S. economy in the postwar period effected a similar process of growth and expansion in the U.S. labor force. The manufacturing sector grew as the size of the industrial working class grew during this period. This expansion on the domestic front continued until the early 1970s. During the decade of the 1970s, a number of factors—among them increasing global rivalry from other capitalist powers such as

Japan and Germany—effected a major shift in production from the domestic front to the international sphere through a shift in the location of production from the United States to the rest of the world—especially the Third World. The accelerated transfer of U.S. capital from the United States to the low-wage areas of the Third World began to have an enormous impact on the composition of the labor force structure, such that a process of decline in size of the manufacturing work force in direct proportion to the decline in the manufacturing sector resulting from the relocation of plants to overseas territories began to take place starting in the early seventies. The consequences of this process of deindustrialization of the United States are numerous but the central dynamic of this process has been the dislocation of the traditional manufacturing work force which has resulted in greater unemployment and underemployment together with a shift from manufacturing employment to service and other tertiary sectors of the economy that pay much lower wages than in manufacturing, hence effecting a consequent drop in the standard of living of workers in the United States over the course of this period to the present.

Between 1970 and 1992, the proportion of workers in goods-producing industries declined from 33.3 percent of the labor force in 1970 to 28.4 percent in 1980, to 22.7 percent in 1990, to 21.6 percent in 1992; in manufacturing industry, it dropped from 27.3 percent in 1970 to 22.4 percent in 1980, to 17.3 percent in 1990, to 16.8 percent in 1992.[8] On the other hand, a segment of the unemployed manufacturing work force that was able to obtain employment in the low-wage service sector accelerated the growth of this sector during the past two decades, such that the proportion of workers in this sector, relative to the total labor force, increased from 66.7 percent in 1970 to 71.6 percent in 1980, to 77.3 percent in 1990, to 78.4 percent in 1992.[9]

The shift in employment from the manufacturing to the service sector over the past two decades has resulted in a decline in real wages of workers by some 20 percent over the past two decades.[10] This has greatly affected the living standard of U.S. workers and forced them to live on lower real income.

A key factor in the decline in purchasing power and living standard for workers in the United States has been a rise in the rate of surplus value (or exploitation) and a consequent drop in labor's share over the years.[11] Thus while both production and productivity per labor hour increased continuously during the postwar period, labor's share drastically fell from 40 percent in 1950 to 25 percent in 1984; at the same time, the rate of surplus value in U.S. manufacturing industry doubled from 150 percent in 1950 to 302 percent in 1984.[12] This, together with favorable government policies toward large corporations, has resulted in record corporate profits. Looking at the past two decades, we find that total net corporate profits more than quadrupled from 1970 to 1988; it rose from $75 billion in 1970 to $200 billion in 1979, to $329 billion in 1988.[13] Likewise, profits of domestic industries increased severalfold during this period, mostly accounted for by nonfinancial industries. Even taking inflation into account—it was quite low in the 1980s—net corporate profits have surged during this period, more than doubling in real terms.[14] An examination of the extent of concentration and centralization of capital, which reveals the extent of monopolization of the economy and thereby the degree of polarization of social classes, indicates that in 1990 some 367 manufacturing corporations with assets totaling $1.9 trillion and net profits of $82 billion accounted for 71 percent of all manufacturing assets and 73 percent of total net profits.[15]

The immense wealth that has been accumulating in the coffers of the capitalist class on the one hand and the continued drop in workers' real wages and living standard on the other has accelerated the polarization of the main classes in American society—labor and capital—and crystallized the growing gap in the distribution of income and wealth in the United States.[16] This is evident in data on the distribution of income in the United States over the past two decades. Thus we find that between 1970 and 1990, while the share in total income of the top 5 percent and the highest fifth of families increased, the share of the bottom three-fifths of families decreased during this same period.[17]

Data on the concentration of wealth in the United States also show the enormous gap between the wealthy and the working class in recent decades. In the 1980s, the richest 10 percent of families owned 78 percent of real estate, 89 percent of corporate stock, over 90 percent of bonds, and 94 percent of all business assets. More significantly, the top .5 percent of all families accounted for nearly or over half of all assets, corporate stock, bonds, and business assets.[18]

As the concentration and centralization of income and wealth moved ahead in full speed during the Reagan years, the continuing class polarization has in the 1990s widened the gap between labor and capital still further and placed the workers into a desperate situation, facing permanent unemployment, indebtedness, economic uncertainty and fear in securing the basic necessities of life, such as food, housing, and health care, for themselves and for their families.

Declining real wages, rising unemployment, growing indebtedness, inability to obtain affordable housing and health care, and a general decline in living standards of workers in the United States during the past two decades have led to increasing impoverishment of the working class both in relative and absolute terms. This situation is now threatening the very survival of millions of workers in providing their families adequate food and shelter to sustain life at the subsistence level.

Finding themselves at such minimum levels of subsistence a growing number of workers have thus been forced to join the ranks of the poverty population which has become a permanent fixture of contemporary American society. The situation was worse in the early 1990s than it was in the

1970s, such that persons below the poverty level increased in number from about twenty-five million during the 1970s to about thirty-six million in the early 1990s.[19] Considering the population living below 125 percent of the poverty level, we find that in the 1970s some thirty-five million people were in this category, while in the early 1990s this number climbed to about forty-eight million.[20] Of the thirty-six million below the poverty level, ten million were African Americans and twenty-four million were whites. In proportionate terms, however, only 11 percent of whites were below the poverty level in 1991, while for African Americans this rate was 33 percent—three times the rate for whites.[21] Likewise, while less than 15 percent of the white population found itself below 125 percent of the poverty level, more than 40 percent of African Americans found themselves below this level. Clearly, a large segment of the working class is seriously affected by poverty, and the effects of racism and sexism have compounded the deteriorating situation of working women and minority workers who have come to suffer disproportionately from the increasing impoverishment of the working class as a whole.

CLASS CONFLICT AND CLASS STRUGGLE IN THE UNITED STATES

Responding to their deteriorating living conditions and to economic uncertainty threatening their jobs and their very being, workers in the United States have resorted to various forms of resistance and struggle against capitalism. In many industries across the country, they have waged important struggles through strikes, walkouts, protests, and other forms of defiance to prove that workers can no longer be taken for granted as subservient tools of capital and capitalist profit.

The limited but real victories achieved in rank-and-file struggles of the past two decades are a beginning for longer-lasting, protracted struggles that require a much more resilient nationwide effort to unleash rank-and-file militancy on an unprecedented scale since the 1930s, so that the 1990s (as were the 1930s) would once again become a decade of militant labor struggles at the grassroots level.

Throughout the 1970s and 1980s workers in many industries across the United States engaged in a large number of strikes, walkouts, and other forms of protest against their employers. Many of the rank-and-file struggles were in fact for the very right to strike—an inalienable right of workers' collective might. The period from the late 1970s on saw intensified rank-and-file struggles in confronting the power of capital at the point of production. Throughout the 1980s more and more workers began to take the initiative on the rungs below to exert their collective strength and fight back to protect their benefits and rights.[22]

Such developments in rank-and-file struggles which intensified at the close of the 1980s have led some labor analysts to express a sense of optimism in the prospects for labor in the 1990s. "In the last years of the eighties," writes labor activist Jane Slaughter, "it has seemed that more and more unionists have been willing to strike or take other dramatic action against their employers."

The Mine Workers called it "class warfare" in southwest Virginia as they battled the Pittston Coal Co., state police, and the courts.

Hundreds of union supporters in International Falls, Minnesota, routed scab construction workers by storming their camp and burning their trailers.

From Eastern Airlines to NYNEX, from contract rejections in the Teamsters to Southern organizing wins by the Amalgamated Clothing Workers, the militancy has caused some in the labor movement to speak hopefully of "an upsurge," even "a turning point."

Many of these struggles received an impressive showing of solidarity from other unionists.[23]

In many unions across the country the late 1980s was also a period of greater rank-and-file demands for union democracy and control. This "upsurge" in rank-and-file activism, Slaughter notes, "is better described as the intensifying of a trend in the labor movement, a trend which is slowly growing and, just as important, which is slowly becoming more conscious of itself."[24]

The development of class consciousness among the working class is not an automatic process, but it *is* nonetheless a direct outcome of the conditions of work and life experienced by millions of workers under capitalism. This process, once fully developed, draws workers into the class struggle—a struggle which is *political* in nature and is waged against the ruling capitalist class and the entire institutional structure of the capitalist system, including the state.[25]

Historically, the central facilitators of the development of class consciousness and class struggle, beyond the narrow economic battles waged through the instrumentality of trade unions at the point of production, have been workers' political associations and parties—that is, organizations of workers that have articulated and advanced the class interests of the working class in a broader political context, with the aim of taking state power away from the capitalists.

The longer history of capitalist development in Europe led at an earlier period to the development of radical workers' organizations of different political persuasions—from anarcho-syndicalist to communist, as well as traditional reformist—as manifested in the Paris Commune, the First International, and later the Bolshevik revolution, among others. Various radical anarcho-syndicalist, socialist, communist, and other labor organizations and parties thus have their origins in these and other struggles of the working class against capitalism in Europe from the late eighteenth to the early twentieth century.[26]

In the United States, the later development of capitalism delayed by a century the emergence of a broad-based workers' struggle against it, but did result in the formation of similar, parallel organizations informed by these collective historic experiences of labor that span over two centuries. By the mid nineteenth century, the U.S. working class had all the signs of a developing mature proletariat ready to take on the system that controlled and exploited them.[27] Playing a critical role in the Civil War and in the victory over the slave system that blocked the further development of its interests in the fight against capitalism in the north, the U.S. working class scored many victories in persistent struggles against the bosses. These struggles resulted in the formation and development of important labor organizations in the late nineteenth and early twentieth centuries: the Knights of Labor, the Industrial Workers of the World, the Socialist and Communist parties, and numerous other politically oriented radical unions and parties were all the outcome of this unfolding process of maturing working-class consciousness and class struggle.[28] Similar struggles during the Great Depression, led by the Communist Party, scored important victories in organizing efforts through unions and political action. The Congress of Industrial Organizations (CIO), for example, worked to improve the condition of labor, while at the same time helped advance working-class consciousness among a growing number of workers in the midst of a great economic catastrophe of rarely seen proportions.[29] "What made the difference in the thirties," writes Gil Green, a veteran labor organizer, "was not only the greater depth of economic and social crisis, but the preparatory work before the conditions of upsurge had fully matured in order to bring them to fruition. The communists and other left-wing militants slowly and methodically began to organize. . . . By their example they proved that organization was possible, and by their policies they helped bring about the necessary unity."[30]

The postwar repression of labor, which through the McCarthyist witch-hunts and expulsions of leftists from the major unions such as the CIO and the UAW effectively set back the labor movement by many years, had a devastating impact on labor's political muscle. It successfully neutralized the influence of organized leftist groups on the labor movement and altered its direction in the conservative fifties—a predicament from which U.S. labor was never able to recover to this day.

The class-collaborationist leadership and policies of the sanitized post-war AFL-CIO officialdom which, in the absence of a strong socialist or communist presence, came to define the nature of "business unionism" wedded to reformist capitalist party-politics rallied behind the Democratic Party, is what distinguishes the current state of the U.S. labor movement from its counterparts in Europe and elsewhere in the advanced capitalist world. The decisive current presence and role of communist, socialist, labor, and other workers' political parties in Europe (and their absence or extreme weakness in the United States) is the chief factor that explains the differential position and prospects of labor in Europe and the United States in recent decades. The existence and strength of an independent workers' political party is, therefore, of crucial importance to labor and the labor movement in its political (class) struggle against capitalism and the capitalist state.

Things are beginning to change on this front, however. There are renewed calls to establish a new, independent workers' party, while other existing older parties and organizations on the left are beginning to mobilize their forces and energies with increasing vigor.[31] As the transformation of the world economy continues and as the internationalization of U.S. capital further weakens the U.S. domestic economy and plunges it into a depressionary crisis in the coming years, hence forcing workers to experience a further decline in their standard of living, there will be increasing pressure from below to mobilize and fight back. The critical factor in this regard will increasingly become the central role of an independent workers' party which will have to take up the task of leading U.S. labor in the class struggle that will surely intensify and spread in the years ahead.

NOTES

1. The only exceptions were Benjamin Franklin (Pennsylvania) and Luther Martin (Maryland). Martin refused to sign the Constitution, and both Martin and Franklin campaigned against the ratification of the Constitution in their respective states.

2. Charles Beard, *An Economic Interpretation of the Constitution of the United States* (New York: Macmillan, 1962). They included James Madison, plantation owner and lawyer; Edmund Randolph of Virginia, owner of 5000 acres and 200 slaves; Robert Morris, the Philadelphia banker; and Gouverneur Morris, land speculator of New York and Philadelphia. Kenneth Neill Cameron, *Humanity and Society: A World History* (New York: Monthly Review Press, 1977), p. 421.

3. Michael Parenti, *Democracy for the Few*, 5th ed. (New York: St. Martin's Press, 1988), p. 67.

4. Herbert Aptheker, *The American Revolution, 1763–1783* (New York: International Publishers, 1960). Women, who constituted half the adult population; slaves, who made up one-fourth of the population; Native Americans; and poor, propertyless whites were not allowed to vote. This, many have argued, is a reflection of the class interests that came to dominate the state after independence.

5. Ibid.

6. Cameron, *Humanity and Society*, p. 421.

7. Albert Szymanski, *The Capitalist State and the Politics of Class* (Cambridge, Mass.: Winthrop, 1978), p. 160.

8. U.S. Council of Economic Advisers, *Economic Report of the President, 1990*, pp. 342–43; *1991*, pp. 404–5; *1993*, pp. 394–95.

9. Ibid.

10. U.S. Council of Economic Advisers, *Economic Report of the President, 1993*, p. 396.

11. Victor Perlo, *Super Profits and Crises: Modern U.S. Capitalism* (New York: International Publishers, 1988), pp. 35–54.

12. Ibid., appendix, table 2A, p. 512.

13. U.S. Council of Economic Advisers, *Economic Report of the President, 1989*, pp. 409–10; *1990*, pp. 395–96.

14. To obtain a more accurate picture of the situation and to calculate the rate of surplus value, however, we need to look at gross profits, for net profits hide the amount of total value created by workers which has already been distributed to other segments of the nonlaboring population, such as in the case of corporate executive salaries; federal, state, and local government taxes; and to numerous other industries and commercial enterprises, such as advertising firms. All these deducted business expenses are paid for from the total surplus value created by the workers.

15. U.S. Bureau of the Census, *Statistical Abstract of the United States, 1992*, p. 540.

16. Denny Braun, *The Rich Get Richer: The Rise of Income Inequality in the United States and the World* (Chicago: Nelson-Hall Publishers, 1991); Jerry Kloby, "Increasing Class Polarization in the United States: The Growth of Wealth and Income Inequality," in Berch Berberoglu (ed.), *Critical Perspectives in Sociology*, 2d ed. (Dubuque, Iowa: Kendall/Hunt Publishing Company, 1993).

17. U.S. Bureau of the Census, *Statistical Abstract of the United States, 1981*, p. 438; *1992*, p. 450.

18. Joint Economic Committee of the U.S. Congress, *The Concentration of Wealth in the United States*, p. 24, cited in Jerry Kloby, "The Growing Divide: Class Polarization in the 1980s," *Monthly Review* 39, no. 4 (September 1987), pp. 4–6.

19. U.S. Bureau of the Census, Current Population Reports, Series P60–185, *Poverty in the United States: 1992* (Washington, D.C.: Government Printing Office, September 1993), p. xi.

20. U.S. Bureau of the Census, *Statistical Abstract of the United States, 1993*, p. 469.

21. Ibid.

22. Rick Fantasia, *Cultures of Solidarity: Consciousness, Action, and Contemporary American Workers* (Berkeley: University of California Press, 1988).

23. Jane Slaughter, "Is the Labor Movement Reaching a Turning Point?" *Labor Notes*, no. 130 (January 1990), p. 7.

24. Ibid., p. 8.

25. Berch Berberoglu, *Political Sociology: A Comparative/Historical Approach* (New York: General Hall, 1990).

26. Ira Katznelson and Al Zolberg (eds.), *Working Class Formation: Nineteenth-century Patterns in Western Europe and the United States* (Princeton, N.J.: Princeton University Press, 1986).

27. Richard Boyer and Herbert Morais, *Labor's Untold Story*, 3rd ed. (New York: United Electrical, Radio & Machine Workers of America, 1980).

28. Ibid.

29. Gil Green, *What's Happening to Labor* (New York: International Publishers, 1976), pp. 27–51; Judith Stepan-Norris and Maurice Zeitlin, " 'Who Gets the Bird?'

or, How the Communists Won Power and Trust in America's Unions," *American Sociological Review* 54 (August 1989).

30. Green, *What's Happening to Labor*, pp. 178–79.

31. See Berch Berberoglu, *The Legacy of Empire: Economic Decline and Class Polarization in the United States* (New York: Praeger, 1992), Chap. 7.

Five

Class Structure of Third World Societies

This chapter examines the class structure of Third World societies that are part of the world capitalist system. Focusing on the dominant mode of production in a variety of social formations, I provide here an analysis of the balance of class forces in Third World societies based on both the prevailing social relations of production and the class nature of the state. Adopting this approach, I explore the development of class relations in different regions of the Third World and show the historical roots of the contemporary capitalist states throughout much of the Third World.[1]

The class forces that have been active in dominating the great majority of societies in the Third World are the large landowners, the local capitalists (consisting of national and comprador segments), and the transnational corporations and their imperial states. The Third World states, controlled by a combination of these class forces, have always protected and advanced the interests of the dominant classes by their repressive bureaucratic state apparatuses.

In many Third World societies the class structure has taken on a neocolonial character. The survival of the state in these societies is based on its role as an appendage of the world capitalist system dominated by the transnational monopolies and the imperial state. Hence, the state in the Third World has become increasingly repressive and authoritarian in order to crush any popular opposition to its role as promoter of the interests of local and transnational ruling classes.[2]

As the dominant classes in these societies have found it necessary to legitimize their increasingly unpopular rule to maintain law and order, to protect private property, and to prevent a revolution against the prevailing social system, the state has adopted a technocratic approach with a focus on capital accumulation and economic growth, combined with severe repression of the working class and other laboring segments of society. Promoting further penetration of the national economy by the transnational monopolies, the neocolonial state has thus played a key role in the internationalization of capital and its predominance in much of the Third World.[3] This process of integration into the world economy has been to a large degree a reaction to a threat posed by the working class to the continued expansion of capitalism in the Third World—one that is becoming an important challenge to both imperialism and local authoritarian regimes.

Elsewhere in the Third World, popular uprisings, based on different alliances of class forces struggling against imperialism and the neocolonial state, have led to state capitalism or socialism. Class forces mobilized by the intermediate sectors of society in state-capitalist formations have seized power by rallying the people around a nationalist ideology directed against imperialism and its internal class allies, the landlords and compradors.[4] In these societies, the state promotes the interests of the local capitalists against imperialism and the transnationals. Despite their differences with neocolonial societies, the class nature of state-capitalist societies nevertheless yields similar results with regard to the exploitation and repression of labor, as capital accumulation (however nationalistically defined) accrues profits and wealth to local capitalists while subjecting the working class to the dictates of state-directed capitalism, the central priority of which is the extraction of surplus value from wage labor.

Revolutions led by worker-peasant alliances against imperialism and local reaction, on the other hand, have resulted in socialism. Unlike neocolonial or state-capitalist societies, socialist societies in the Third World have taken up as their priority the abolition of the exploitation of labor for private profit and the redistribution of land, property, and income to elevate the living standards of the masses.

These variants of Third World societies have developed out of the complex relations within and between states in the Third World and between them and the imperial centers ever since the advent of colonialism and imperialism which, over time, planted the seeds of capitalism in these societies.

The development of capitalism in the Third World has been uneven, chiefly because of variations in local precapitalist modes of production but also as a result of the nature and duration of contact with other capitalist formations. This process took place during the period of Western colonialism and imperialism on a world scale, which began to expand in the sixteenth century. The changes effected by this interaction yielded different results in different regions of the Third World and led to alternative paths of development in the Caribbean, Latin America, Africa, Asia, and the Middle East. This, in turn, facilitated the emergence and development of varied forms of capitalism and capitalist class structures throughout the Third World.

THE ORIGINS OF THIRD WORLD CLASS SYSTEMS: HISTORICAL BACKGROUND

The history of Third World class systems goes back a number of centuries to the despotic empires that gave rise to class divisions and led to the subsequent emergence of various forms of class societies. The transformation of indigenous empires in the aftermath of European expansion to the Americas as well as Africa, Asia, and other regions of the world led to establishing feudal and later capitalist class structures in these regions. To develop a better understanding of the origins and development of class systems in each of these regions, we shall take a closer look at the history of each region in class terms.

Prior to European expansion to the New World in the sixteenth century, the dominant mode of production in much of Central and South America was tributary, as in the Incan, Aztec, and Mayan empires, where the state played a dominant role. The central state, which had ultimate property rights, was the leading force in society, while peasants living in village communities were obliged to pay tribute to the state. In North America, parts of the Caribbean, and some areas of South America, the tribal or primitive communal mode of production predominated among indigenous peoples. These societies were classless and relied on hunting, fishing, gathering, and some early forms of horticulture for their subsistence. Lack of a substantial surplus and relative distance from aggressive empires prevented them from evolving toward a tributary mode through the emergence or imposition of a parasitic state. These formations remained intact until the arrival of the European colonizers in the early sixteenth century, which brought about major transformations in the social structure of tributary and tribal societies throughout the New World.

The colonization of the Americas began at a time when Spain was in transition from feudalism to capitalism, with feudalism still dominant. Spanish expansion into the New World was characterized by plunder of the newly acquired colonies. The Spanish military leaders who conquered the Indian territories were granted the right to collect tribute or obtain labor services from the local populations. This system of labor relations throughout most of Spanish America came to be known as the *encomienda* system.[5] Essentially it meant that the conquering state (Spain) replaced the empires previously dominant over the native territories, although it upheld the tributary mode that served the feudal (and increasingly capitalist) Spanish state in its worldwide expansion to secure precious metals and luxury goods for the ruling classes of Europe. During the initial stage of plunder, the colonies became an appendage of Spain without undergoing a major transformation in their mode of production or class structure.

As the Indian population declined, as a result of the plunder, and Spain accelerated its acquisition of new land, it became necessary to secure Indian labor to work the land. The system of *repartimiento* (*corvée* labor), which allocated Indian workers to Spanish estates (*haciendas*), came to supplant the *encomienda*. Under the new system, Indians were required to work on the *haciendas* on a rotational basis for specific periods of time. Gradually, European forms of feudal relations were introduced as Indians became permanently bound serfs on the *haciendas*. This was facilitated by the destruction of native irrigation systems, the incorporation of native land into Spanish estates, and the forced evacuation of Indians from their land.[6] The subservience of the natives to the new landowning class ushered in a period of lord-serf relations similar to those practiced in Spain. Feudal relations of production were dominant throughout much of Spanish America until the early nineteenth century.[7]

Elsewhere, in Brazil, an insufficient number of Indians necessitated the importation of slaves from Africa. Thus feudal Portugal set up slavery as the dominant mode of production in its Brazilian colony in order to facilitate the extraction of precious metals and other raw materials for sale on the world market. Slaves were used first in sugarcane fields and later in mining gold and diamonds. This continued until the late eighteenth century when slavery was abolished and the ex-slaves became proto-serfs—they still worked their master's land but had some rights granted to them. Sharecropping developed alongside these feudal relations and, with the expansion of an export sector and later capitalist agriculture, wage labor as well.

In the Caribbean and along the Atlantic coast of North America, a similar pattern was established. Black slaves from Africa worked the sugar and cotton plantations, while the indigenous peoples of these areas were displaced or physically eliminated, thus transforming local social structures.[8] In these regions, the British colonialists became the dominant force.

The colonial expansion of Europe not only transformed the mode of production in the New World through the introduction of slavery and feudalism, but also facilitated the development of capitalism in Europe and led to its later spread to the colonies. With the development of European capitalism in the eighteenth century, trade with the colonies increasingly took on a capitalist character. As a result, alongside the feudal landowning class in the colonies, a class of merchants developed, tied to the world market controlled by European commercial interests. In time, some of these merchants expanded into industrial pursuits and set the basis for capitalist development. Small-scale manufacturing, based on wage labor, began to take root in the colonies and provided an outlet for capital accumulation among a section of the propertied classes. Nevertheless, the feudal landowning class and its political ally the commercial capitalists remained the dominant economic and political forces in the colonies even after independence.[9]

In the early nineteenth century, whereas the main sources of wealth in Latin America were controlled by the local propertied classes, political power was still monopolized by the Spanish crown. This division of economic and political control of Latin American colonies served as the principal source of conflict between the local industrial capitalists and the colonial center, Spain.

The independence movement of the nineteenth century was an attempt to obtain political autonomy from Spain. From 1830 to 1880, most of the newly formed nations of Latin America underwent a series of brutal civil wars. The industrial capitalists and their nationalist allies on the one side and the commercial and landowning classes tied to the colonial center on the other opposed each other in a seemingly perpetual battle that lasted for decades. In the end, the latter emerged victorious and set the stage for the subsequent development of Latin American society and class structure on a neocolonial capitalist path tied to various colonial and imperial centers throughout the nineteenth and twentieth centuries.

In Africa, prior to European intervention, a diverse social structure existed based on various modes of production in different regions of the continent. The primitive communal mode was dominant in some areas, and the Asiatic and feudal modes were paramount in others. Although slavery was practiced in various parts of the continent before the European-initiated slave trade, it never became a dominant mode of production in precolonial Africa. Primitive communal relations of production were prevalent in central and parts of southern Africa, while the Asiatic mode dominated much of North Africa until the end of the nineteenth century. Feudalism in various forms was practiced in parts of East and West Africa.[10]

Despite the prevalence of these diverse modes in various parts of the continent, precolonial Africa consisted in large part of self-sufficient village communities engaged in subsistence agriculture. Where feudalism or a despotic state existed, villagers provided a surplus to the ruling classes in the form of tribute or a part of their produce. With the widespread introduction of the slave trade by European imperialism, greater stratification was induced in the continent, and many newly created tribal chiefs were corrupted by European conquerors and turned into tyrants serving the interests of Western imperialism. The artificial creation of "district chiefs" in the French colonies and of "headmen" in the English colonies was done for this purpose.[11] After the sixteenth century, when the world economy facilitated the spread of the slave trade in Africa, slaves became Africa's major export. They were bought and sold to masters in various parts of the world, especially in the Americas.

The slave trade inhibited indigenous capital accumulation and thus the development of local capitalism, as it deprived Africa of able-bodied workers, undermined local artisan production because of the cheap European goods received for the slaves, and reinforced slavery as a mode of production. The economic development that did take place during this period was highly dependent on the European colonial economy tied to the slave trade.[12] With the end of the slave trade in the first half of the nineteenth century, African economies shifted to commercial export crops. Commodities such as cocoa, peanuts, palm oil, coffee, and rubber became the principal exports. As a result, the previously dominant ruling classes, whose wealth and power were based on the slave trade, transformed themselves into planters who imposed semifeudal production relations on their ex-slaves, who now labored on vast plantations in serflike conditions. The wealth and power of the local ruling class declined during the course of the nineteenth century as European colonialism gained a more direct foothold in the continent and became involved in production and trade throughout the area.

By the end of the nineteenth century, the European powers had moved in with full force against local states and chiefdoms and set up colonial regimes. Labor migration became the main mechanism to secure a labor force in the mining sector, as well as in commercial crop production. Africans engaged in subsistence production on communal lands were manipulated into providing labor to the Europeans, who introduced taxes payable in money. In this way they were able to force Africans to work in European-owned enterprises to secure the means to pay their taxes. At the same time, labor services (*corvée*) were introduced, although they could often be avoided in exchange for a cash payment. To avoid *corvée*, one had to prove gainful employment. Either way, the European colonialists were the only ones to gain from these practices.

In time, the notion of private property was introduced, which undermined traditional subsistence agriculture and led to increased demands for commercial goods. This provided sufficient incentive to get Africans to sell their labor power for a wage. Over time, the African economies became increasingly commercial, wage labor became more prevalent, raw material exports grew, and the demand for European industrial imports increased. As a result, Africa evolved along the capitalist path tied to the European-dominated world economy, which at the end of the nineteenth and beginning of the twentieth centuries had transformed Africa by introducing capitalist relations of production into the continent through colonial rule.

The different forms of exploitation and the different class structures that developed during the colonial era in Latin America, Africa, and elsewhere can thus be explained in terms of the different modes of production prevailing in Europe and in the colonies, as well as the interaction between them at different points in history. In this sense, the precapitalist imperialism of

Spain in Latin America and other colonial regions produced a legacy of feudalism that lingers today, while the capitalist imperialism of a more developed industrial Europe in transition to monopoly capital at a later period produced a qualitatively different result in Africa, as well as in parts of Asia, where capitalist relations of production began to take root.[13]

Vast areas of Asia were colonized by Western powers until the middle of the twentieth century. British and European imperialism mercilessly plundered these regions at the height of their empires. Through their presence in the area, they effected major changes in the social and economic structures of the societies of Asia they came to dominate. As in Latin America, feudal relations of production were introduced in Spain's Asian colony, the Philippines; the slave mode was introduced and despotic rule was reinforced in Java and other parts of colonial Indonesia by the Dutch; and capitalism made headway in British India and British-controlled parts of Southeast Asia. Although not formally colonized, China too came under the influence and control of the Western powers, as traditional forms of exploitation were reinforced through the link to Europe and other centers of Western imperialism.

Before the arrival of colonial and imperial powers, many Asian societies evolved within the framework of an Oriental despotic system where the Asiatic mode of production was dominant. With the expansion of Europe to remote corners of Asia, these societies came into contact with and were transformed by different colonizers. Thus the results were different in British colonies from those in colonies held by Spain, Holland, France, or other colonial powers. While today the remnants of semifeudal relations are the product of an earlier phase of colonial transformation, capitalism and capitalist relations were introduced in later periods of imperial expansion.

Prior to British rule, the dominant mode of production in India was tributary. Unlike European feudalism, land in India did not belong to any private landlord; the state was the supreme owner of the soil. The central authority, the king, delegated to some persons the right of *zamin*, or the right to collect revenues for the state. The *zamindars* were intermediaries between the communal villages and the state, and had no rights over the land. In return for their function as tax collectors, the *zamindars* were given a share of the taxes they collected.[14] Later, with British rule in the late eighteenth century, the *zamindars* emerged as an independent class with full rights in the ownership of land. In some parts of India, such as Bengal, the British decreed that the *zamindars* were to be considered landlords, thus creating a class of large landowners with inheritable ownership rights in the land. Elsewhere in India (e.g., in the south), the British considered the peasants to have ownership rights in the land and collected taxes from them directly. As a result, this section of the country saw the development of the small landholding. During the course of the nineteenth century, market forces led to an increasing concentration of wealth and gave rise to a large landowning class on the one hand, and renters, sharecroppers, rural laborers, or urban proletarians on the other. British entry into India accelerated the activities of merchants as well; they were to become the intermediaries through whom the British would control the local economy. Engaged in import-export trade and incorporated into the world capitalist system, these merchants became the equivalent of the comprador capitalists. Through both the landlords and the compradors, who together constituted the local ruling classes (tied to a weakened central state), the British were able to preserve the existing order and protect and advance their interests.[15]

Thus, while the domination of a class of landlords in the countryside ensured the development of feudal or semifeudal relations of production in agriculture in some parts of the country (and the emergence of capitalist relations through wage labor in other parts), the growth of merchant's capital led to the development of an urban commercial economy tied to Britain through international trade.[16] As trade with Britain increased, and the demand for Indian goods grew, local capital expanded into crafts, textiles, and industrial production. This gave rise to a renewed expansion of local manufacturing industry and with it the development of a national capitalist class that came to be seen as a competitor of British imperialism. This prompted Britain to take steps to crush Indian industry and turn India into an appendage of Britain's colonial economy.[17] Antagonism between British and local industrial capital led to the national capitalist alliance with the peasantry to throw off the British yoke through the independence movement.[18] Much as in North America, but unlike the situation in Latin America, the national capitalist forces were able to consolidate power and capture the leadership of the movement in a victory over the British. By the late 1940s, they installed a state committed to developing national capitalism in India following independence. Given the relatively weak position of the local capitalists, the victorious national forces were able to utilize the powers of the state and establish a state capitalist regime to assist the accumulation of capital by the Indian capitalist class.[19]

China's experience in state formation has been markedly different from that of India. Until the nineteenth century, China was ruled by a series of despotic states under successive dynasties, but the imperial state was relatively weak and depended on private landlords who owned vast tracts of land.[20] The widespread presence of private property in the means of production in Imperial China meant that it was not dominated by the Asiatic mode of production. But the private landlords did not have sufficient control of the state to turn it into an instrument of feudal rule; a fairly strong state bureaucracy maintained relative autonomy from the landlord class and exercised its rule over society as a whole. Thus it would likewise be erroneous to characterize Chinese society at this time as feudal.

During the imperial epoch, China possessed a despotic state, within the boundaries of which existed a landed nobility, a merchant class, petty commodity producers (consisting of peasants and artisans), and hired laborers. The economic strength of an already developed landed gentry, by way of its access to and control over a significant portion of the means of production, compelled the state to share power with the landlords over the peasants and landless laborers from whom they extracted a share of the surplus in the form of taxes, produce, and/or rent. Within this framework of domination under a semi-Asiatic/semifeudal mode, a merchant class tied to overseas trade flourished.

The capital accumulated from trade was gradually invested in crafts and manufacturing production and, together with a merger with expanding artisan elements in basic home industries, led to the development of a national capitalist class. At the same time, some peasants were able to improve their lot and accumulate sufficient wealth to constitute a rich peasant class (similar to *kulaks*). Others lost their land to large landowners, ending up either working for them as rural laborers or migrating to the cities and becoming wage workers. These parallel developments in city and countryside strengthened the development of feudalism and capitalism throughout China and laid the basis for the transformation of Chinese society following the disintegration of the central state. With the landlords allied with commercial interests in firm control of the state, China entered a period of feudal rule and later evolved toward capitalism.

By the end of the eighteenth and beginning of the nineteenth centuries, Western powers had begun to intervene in China and attempted to incorporate it into the world capitalist system.[21] A protracted struggle against Western imperialism followed, and ushered in a period of intense nationalism that paved the way for the national capitalist forces to capture state power by the early twentieth century. Remaining within the world capitalist system and unable to suppress internal reaction, the nationalist government of Sun Yat-Sen was considerably weakened. Taking advantage of the situation, the reactionary anticommunist forces within the Kuomintang, under the leadership of Chiang Kai-shek, captured power and imposed an iron rule over China that led to a long and bloody civil war during which thousands of communists and revolutionaries were executed. The betrayal of the national-democratic, anti-imperialist revolution by the rightists in the Kuomintang, who embraced imperialism to crush the growing working-class and communist movements, led to the reemergence of an independent communist movement based on a worker-peasant alliance under the leadership of the Chinese Communist Party headed by Mao Zedong. After a long struggle against Japanese and U.S. imperialism and through the mobilization of millions of workers and peasants during the 1930s and 1940s, the Chinese masses triumphed in a communist-led revolution in 1949 that brought to an end feudalist-capitalist exploitation and imperialist plunder and launched a new, people's democracy through the institution of a socialist state. Thus was born the People's Republic of China.

The historical development of Third World class systems examined above illustrates the rich diversity of class structures and class struggles across Latin America, Africa, Asia, and other regions of the Third World. They show the unique interaction of internal and external social processes that came to define the nature and structure of class forces that constitute the class structure of Third World societies today.

THE CONTEMPORARY CLASS STRUCTURE OF THIRD WORLD SOCIETIES

The class structures of most Third World societies today are defined by capitalist relations of production based on the exploitation of wage labor. This is so throughout Latin America and much of Asia, Africa, and the Middle East. The expansion of capitalism and capitalist class relations in the Third World have been facilitated by imperialism through the internationalization of capital and capitalist relations of production.

During the height of British imperialism in the late nineteenth century, most Latin American economies were penetrated by British finance capital. Such penetration manifested itself in the direct control of raw materials by British interests. The investment of foreign capital in the Latin economies consequently integrated the national capitalist classes into the global economic system in such a way that most Latin American countries became semicolonies of the expanding British Empire.

The outbreak of major global crises during the first half of the twentieth century brought about important changes in the external relations and internal structures of the majority of Latin American countries. The disruption of world trade during World War I was to be intensified by the Great Depression of the 1930s and by World War II. The decline in foreign trade and foreign capital substantially weakened Latin America's economic ties with Britain. These changes in the structure of the world economy created economic conditions and allowed political changes in Latin America that were to begin the region's strongest nationalist policy and largest independent industrialization drive since the 1830s. The drive subsequently opened for the Latin American industrial capitalists the period of import-substituting industrialization directed toward the diversification of the production structure in manufactures. International crises thus freed Latin America from outright subordination to imperial centers and accelerated its growth toward independent capitalist development. During this period, most Latin American societies came under the control of the national capitalists, whose interests dictated the development of a strong capitalist state.

The ascendancy of the United States in the Western hemisphere after World War II—a result of Britain's declining economic power and near defeat during the war—effected the interimperialist transfer of control over Latin America from Britain to the United States. During the 1950s, as the United States began to rely increasingly on strategic raw materials from abroad, U.S. economic expansion into Latin America accelerated. The need for metals and minerals brought about a rapid expansion of U.S. investment in Latin America in subsequent decades. However, by the mid 1960s the pattern of U.S. economic penetration in the hemisphere had taken on new forms, as U.S.-based transnational corporations began to penetrate the national industries of Latin America and to control the manufacturing sector developed by the local industrial capitalists.[22] As a result, the independent industrialization process initiated by the national capitalists in the more advanced countries of the region in the 1930s was gradually transformed, and their economies became an appendage of the world capitalist economy dominated by the U.S. monopolies. Moving them in the direction of export-oriented satellites as they fulfilled their role in the new international division of labor, the economic changes effected by this new relationship required the introduction of political changes as well. Repressive military rule was needed to stabilize the existing social order and the "democratic" capitalist states of an earlier period thus gave way to the authoritarian and repressive neocolonial states, followed by a transition to civilian rule orchestrated by the military. Capitalist development in Latin America in the postwar period consequently brought about a transformation in the balance of class forces and transferred state power into the hands of comprador elements tied to the transnational corporations and the U.S. imperial state. This transfer of political power in a neocolonial direction had an immense impact on the class structure of Latin American societies.

In Africa, until the middle of the twentieth century, when most African countries won their formal independence, the local economies were a direct appendage of the colonial center, which directed development in the colonies. The pattern was based on the logic of the capitalist mode of production that dominated the economies of the center states and evolved according to its needs of accumulation, resulting in uneven development between the imperial center and the colonies, and within the colonies. In general, most African colonies specialized in one or a few raw materials for export and depended on the import of finished manufactured goods from the imperial center.

This classic colonial relationship prevailed in a number of African countries after the granting of formal independence, and led to the restructuring of social-economic relations on a neocolonial basis. This has been the case throughout much of the continent.[23] As in the colonial period, the main characteristic of these neocolonial states is their heavy reliance on the export of raw materials to the advanced capitalist countries and the import of finished manufactured goods from them.[24]

Within this neocolonial structure, there has nevertheless occurred a parallel development of transnational corporate expansion into the manufacturing sector of some of these countries in order to utilize cheap labor in a variety of manufacturing and industrial undertakings. This has contributed to the growth of the industrial sector and effected changes in the sectoral distribution of the gross domestic product in favor of industry. As a result, the share of industry relative to agriculture has increased over time.[25] Despite the fact that the pace of industrialization in these countries is considerably slower than in Latin America and East and Southeast Asia, the move in the direction of investments in industry has brought about a significant change in the economic and labor force structure of these countries and placed them on the road to further capitalist development within the boundaries of the world economy. Thus, while neocolonial African states continue to remain primarily agricultural or raw-material-exporting countries, the relative growth of manufacturing and other industry vis-à-vis agriculture indicates an overall trend toward industrialization within a neocolonial framework tied to imperialism.

Elsewhere in Africa, nationalist forces have taken the initiative to lead the newly independent states along a less dependent path. Utilizing the military and state bureaucracy as supportive institutions to carry out their development programs, nationalist leaders in these countries have opted for a state-capitalist path in line with their class vision of society and social-economic development. Unlike neocolonial states, the national state-capitalist formations of Africa became the leading progressive force on the continent in the initial decades of the postcolonial period. On the economic front, these regimes made significant progress in industrialization, as the share of industry in the Gross Domestic Product (GDP) of these countries reached impressive levels relative to agriculture and other sectors of the economy. This was reflected in the labor force structure as well, with a general trend of decline in the proportion of the labor force in agriculture and steady increase in the labor force in industry. However, because state power remained in the hands of technocrats and intellectuals without a base in the working class, imperialist pressures from the outside eventually derailed the state-directed nationalist project and led to the gradual adoption of neocolonial policies in conformity with the world economy. The limited internal social transformations initiated earlier were gradually eroded in order to meet international commercial and financial obligations resulting from ties with imperialism.[26] This, in turn, increasingly led these societies in a neocolonial direction.

On the other hand, in countries where workers and peasants have played an active role in the struggle for liberation against colonialism and imperialism (such as in Angola, Mozambique, and Zimbabwe), strides have been made toward genuine economic and political independence, accompanied by deep social transformations with progress toward socialism. With political power in the hands of workers, peasants, and intellectuals committed to advancing the interests of the masses, these countries have progressed in all facets of social-economic life, despite the enormous international (imperialist) and regional South African (colonial/racist) encroachments into their territories.

The volatile nature of the southern African triangle, including the progressive revolutionary regimes of Angola, Mozambique, and Zimbabwe on the borders of apartheid South Africa, has had a major impact on the scope and pace of socialist development, proving once again the difficulty of building socialism in the midst of hostile imperialist forces intent on blocking its development. The winds of change are blowing throughout the continent, however, most fervently in South Africa. A major revolutionary explosion in that country in the aftermath of the collapse of the apartheid system could well trigger upheaval throughout the continent, thus changing the face of Africa.

In Asia, following World War II a number of societies emerged as appendages of the world capitalist system. Evolving as neocolonies of the expanding U.S. empire in the postwar period, these societies came to serve the economic and strategic interests of U.S. monopolies in providing cheap labor, raw materials, new markets, new investment outlets, and a military outpost throughout the region. From South Korea and Taiwan to the Philippines, Vietnam, and Indonesia, the countries that came under the U.S. grip served one or more of the above functions and provided the material base for U.S. transnational expansion in the region. By the early 1950s and subsequently, these countries, together with defeated Japan, came under the U.S. military umbrella in the Pacific Basin and provided a foundation for the expansion of U.S. transnational corporations.

With the expansion of U.S. capital in East and Southeast Asia in the 1960s and 1970s, these regions became more fully integrated into the world economy. Through such investments, and other economic arrangements, these societies came to fulfill their special role in the international division of labor controlled by the United States. This prompted a rapid expansion of capitalism in these countries through increased foreign investment and subcontracting with local firms to fill transnational orders destined for markets in advanced capitalist countries.[27]

But this transnational-directed industrialization process exacerbated larger social and economic problems confronting these countries while creating minimal employment at very low wages and draining the profits made from the sale of exported goods. Moreover, to assure the compliance of the local population, the forces benefiting from this plunder put in place instruments of political repression through the installation of brutal (often military) dictatorships that have violated basic human rights.

The social significance of transnational capitalist expansion in these regions lies in the transformation of local relations of production in a capitalist direction and the consolidation of a capitalist state tied to imperialism, with all its inherent class contradictions. The increase in size of the working class in the manufacturing sector and, more broadly, in all major branches of industry, accompanied by below-subsistence wages and antilabor legislation enacted by repressive neocolonial states, have led to the intensification of the class struggle in these societies, with some of them reaching a near-revolutionary stage, as the masses challenge the rule of the neocolonial capitalist states in East Asia and other regions of the Third World.

NATIONAL LIBERATION AND CLASS STRUGGLE IN THE THIRD WORLD

The worldwide expansion of international capital during the course of this century, especially since World War II, has led to struggles between labor and capital on a world scale. Class struggles, together with anti-imperialist national liberation struggles have intensified in regions and countries of the world where imperialism has made the greatest headway.

In Latin America they are the relatively more developed and larger countries of Brazil, Mexico, and Argentina, and increasingly Peru, Chile, Venezuela, and a number of countries in Central America and the Caribbean region. These struggles, in the form of strikes, demonstrations, mass protests, and a variety of direct and indirect political actions, have intensified in recent years, in some countries reaching a critical stage.

In Africa, too, class struggles are unfolding with exceptional speed. The popular forces fighting for national liberation and social revolution are waging a determined struggle to rid themselves of neocolonial bondage chained to the transnational monopolies and the imperial state. From Morocco, Tunisia, and Egypt in the north, to Sudan, Kenya, and Uganda in the east, to Ghana and Nigeria in the west, to apartheid South Africa in the south, workers and the oppressed are rising up to take charge of their own destinies. Inspired by victories in Angola, Mozambique, and Zimbabwe, the working people of Africa are struggling to liberate themselves from imperialism and neocolonialism.

The strong presence of Western, especially United States, dominance in Asia has prompted a wave of uprisings throughout the region in recent decades—from Indonesia to Thailand, to South Korea, and to the Philippines. The repressive state policies prevailing in these countries today— most visibly in South Korea—are leading more and more laboring people to join in the mass struggle against imperialism and the local authoritarian capitalist state. Given the recent history of labor struggles and the generally politicized nature of the work force in these and other countries of Asia, such popular mobilization has resulted in the creation of conditions leading to protracted class struggles and large-scale social transformations that are yet to come.[28]

Given the politicized nature of the prevailing conditions in Latin America, Asia, Africa, and other regions of the Third World, such struggles have the potential to topple governments, local ruling classes, and imperialism, and alter the existing neocolonial capitalist order. Strikes, demonstrations, and mass protests initiated by workers and other segments of the population have become frequent in a growing number of countries controlled by imperialism. The working people are rising up against the local ruling classes, the state, and the transnational monopolies that have together effected the super-exploitation of labor for decades. Varied forms of class struggle on the one hand and the struggle for national liberation led by the working class on the other are two sides of the same process of struggle for the transformation of society now underway in many countries under the grip of foreign capital.

The logic of transnational expansion on a world scale is such that it leads to the emergence and development of forces in conflict with this expansion. When we consider the totality of the political forces at work in the Third World, we see that the working class has been in the forefront of these struggles. Strikes, mass demonstrations, political protest, confrontation with the local client state, armed insurrection, civil war, and revolutionary upheavals are all part and parcel of the contradictory nature of relations imposed on the laboring people by imperialism and its client states throughout the Third World. The material conditions that have led to U.S. imperialist domination of the world economy up to the present period have now reached a point where broad segments of the masses in the Third World are coming together to challenge it at its very foundations.

CONCLUSION

Our analysis of the historical development of class structures in different regions of the Third World indicates the varied nature and development of Third World societies that have evolved out of interaction between local precapitalist modes with capitalism that originated in Europe and other colonial and imperial centers of the world economy.

Prevailing in much of the less-developed capitalist world, the comprador-capitalist dominated states constitute the bulk of capitalist societies in the Third World today. With the spread of capitalism and capitalist relations in the Third World, state power has increasingly come under the influence and later control of the comprador capitalists, as the traditional alliance of landlords and compradors has given way to the further expansion of the economic interests of the local bourgeoisie collaborating with imperialism. The transformation of the internal social structure of comprador-capitalist states has been most visible in countries receiving the greatest amount of foreign manufacturing investments since the early 1960s. Largely as a result of these investments, a high rate of growth has occurred in the manufacturing sector, signifying the new relationship between local comprador capitalists and imperialism as these countries have come to serve the special needs of the transnational monopolies, especially the need for cheap labor. While this pattern of development has accelerated the spread of capitalist production relations in these countries, it has also given rise to the growth of an increasingly militant working class that is beginning to challenge the prevailing comprador-capitalist power structure.

The variation in the class structure of different Third World formations tells us something about the effects generated by the relations between imperialism and dominant class forces. These relations reinforce a development pattern that on the one hand perpetuates existing class structures, and on the other it sets the conditions for the transformation of society, thus affecting the class structure and the form of the state in a variety of societies throughout the Third World.

NOTES

1. This chapter is based on my earlier studies of class structure in the Third World. See Berch Berberoglu, *The Internationalization of Capital* (New York: Praeger, 1987), part 2; idem, *Political Sociology* (New York: General Hall, 1990), chap. 6; and idem, *The Political Economy of Development* (Albany, N.Y.: State University of New York Press, 1992), part 3.

2. Albert Szymanski, *The Logic of Imperialism* (New York: Praeger, 1981), chap. 13.

3. Ibid. See also Berberoglu, *The Internationalization of Capital*, chap. 7.

4. On state capitalism in the Third World, see Berch Berberoglu, "The Nature and Contradictions of State Capitalism in the Third World," *Social and Economic Studies* 28, no. 2 (1980).

5. Stanley J. Stein and Barbara H. Stein, *The Colonial Heritage of Latin America* (New York: Oxford University Press, 1970).

6. Ibid.

7. Ernesto Laclau, "Feudalism and Capitalism in Latin America," *New Left Review* 67 (May-June 1971).

8. Eric Williams, *Capitalism and Slavery* (New York: Capricorn, 1966).

9. Laclau, "Feudalism and Capitalism in Latin America."

10. Feudalism practiced in these regions, especially in East Africa, however, was based mainly on control of cattle, rather than of land, as in Europe.

11. See Richard Harris, ed., *The Political Economy of Africa* (Cambridge, Mass.: Schenkman, 1975).

12. Basil Davidson, *The African Slave Trade* (Boston: Little, Brown, 1961).

13. See Berch Berberoglu, "Pre-Capitalist Modes of Production: Their Origins, Contradictions, and Transformation," *Quarterly Review of Historical Studies* 19, nos. 1–2 (1980).

14. See Anupam Sen, *The State, Industrialization, and Class Formations in India* (London: Routledge & Kegan Paul, 1982).

15. Berch Berberoglu, ed., *India: National Liberation and Class Struggles* (Meerut, India: Sarup & Sons, 1986).

16. Sen, *The State, Industrialization, and Class Formations in India.*

17. Hamza Alavi, "India and the Colonial Mode of Production," *Economic and Political Weekly*, August 1975.

18. See Bipan Chandra, "The Indian Capitalist Class and Imperialism Before 1947," *Journal of Contemporary Asia* 5, no. 3 (1975).

19. A. I. Levkovsky, *Capitalism in India* (Delhi: People's Publishing House, 1966).

20. Frances V. Moulder, *Japan, China and the Modern World Economy* (Cambridge: Cambridge University Press, 1977), pp. 60–62.

21. Ibid., pp. 98–127.

22. Analysis of the evolution of U.S. direct investment in Latin American manufacturing industries reveals that capital held by parent companies rose from $780 million in 1950 to $4.2 billion in 1970 to $25.7 billion in 1992. U.S. Department of Commerce, *Survey of Current Business* 73, No. 7 (July 1993), p. 100.

23. Colin Leys, *Underdevelopment in Kenya* (Berkeley: University of California Press, 1975); Mahmood Mamdani, *Politics and Class Formation in Uganda* (New York: Monthly Review Press, 1976).

24. For a fuller discussion on this, see Berberoglu, "The Contradictions of Export-Oriented Development in the Third World," *Social and Economic Studies* 36, no. 4 (December 1987), pp. 106–10.

25. World Bank, *World Development Report, 1983* (Washington, D.C.: Oxford University Press, 1983), pp. 152–53.

26. See Karen Farsoun, "State Capitalism in Algeria," *MERIP Reports*, no. 35 (1975); and Issa G. Shivji, *Class Struggles in Tanzania* (New York: Monthly Review Press, 1976).

27. See Martin Landsberg, "Export-Led Industrialization in the Third World: Manufacturing Imperialism," *Review of Radical Political Economics* 11, no. 4 (Winter 1979). See also Bill Warren, *Imperialism, Pioneer of Capitalism* (London: Verso, 1980). Warren argues that imperialism, in the form of overseas investments, promotes the development of capitalism and capitalist relations, regardless of its point of origin and deformed character.

28. See, for example, Martin Landsberg, "South Korea: The 'Miracle' Rejected," *Critical Sociology* 15, No. 3 (Fall, 1988); and idem, *The Rush to Development* (New York: Monthly Review Press, 1993). W. Olson, "Crisis and Social Change in Mexico's Political Economy," *Latin American Perspectives* 46 (1985), pp. 7–28; Frederick Deyo, Stephen Heggard, and Hagen Koo, "Labor in the Political Economy of East Asian Industrialization," *Bulletin of Concerned Asian Scholars* 19, no. 2 (April-June, 1987); Clive Hamilton, *Capitalist Industrialization in Korea* (Boulder, Col.: Westview Press, 1986).

Six

Class, Nation, and State: Nationalism and Class Struggle

Nationalism, once thought of as a historical phenomenon emerging with the rise of capitalism and the nation-state in Europe during the eighteenth century, has more recently reemerged as a manifestation of struggles for national liberation and self-determination in countries and regions of the Third World that have been dominated by colonialism and imperialism in this century.[1] Today, in the final decade of the twentieth century, nationalism has become a worldwide phenomenon, spreading to every corner of the globe—from the Middle East to Southern Africa, to Europe, to North America, and to the former Soviet Union. That such nationalist fervor should develop in an age of internationalism, when the internationalization of capital has torn down national and geographic boundaries and ushered in the era of an interdependent world political economy, is hardly surprising, given the fact that there still remain a number of unresolved national questions that embody the struggles of peoples for national liberation and self-determination, whatever their political form or class content.[2]

This chapter examines the origins and development of nationalism and national movements and provides an analysis of the class nature of these phenomena within the framework of the relationship between class, nation, and state—an analysis that situates nationalism and national movements within the context of class relations and class struggles.

ORIGINS OF NATIONALISM AND NATIONAL MOVEMENTS

Originating in Europe in a period when the rising European bourgeoisie in the eighteenth century found it necessary to establish nation-states to protect their economic interests and thus consolidate their class rule,[3] the phenomenon of nation and nationalism became the political expression of rival capitalist powers engaged in a life-and-death struggle for world domination throughout the eighteenth and nineteenth centuries.

In the twentieth century, nationalism and national movements have emerged across much of the world as rallying points in the context of the struggle against European colonialism and imperialism.[4] National struggles against foreign domination in Asia, Africa, and the Middle East, for example, have taken the form of anticolonial or anti-imperialist liberation struggles—as in India and China in the 1940s, in Algeria and Cuba in the 1950s, and in much of sub-Saharan Africa in the 1960s.[5] In these and other countries and regions of the Third World subjected to external domination, the yearning for national independence and self-determination has taken the form of political struggles to establish sovereign national states with jurisdiction over a national territory based on self-rule.

We have seen such movements develop in a variety of settings in the Third World—from secular political struggles for a homeland (as in Palestine), to regional and cultural autonomy and self-rule across several states (as in Kurdistan), to struggles to end racism and national oppression (as in apartheid South Africa). A multitude of national, political, cultural, and religious conflicts in the context of larger regional military confrontations have surfaced even in modernizing secular states, such as Lebanon, where the resurgence of national, ethnic, and fundamentalist religious movements have led to social strife and civil war.[6] Elsewhere, in the advanced capitalist countries, movements of previously colonized peoples and territories (such as Puerto Rico) and of oppressed groups and nationalities (as in Northern Ireland, the Basque Provinces, and Quebec) have emerged and developed during this century, especially during the past several decades. In the socialist countries, especially in the former Soviet Union, nationalist movements have sprung up in the Baltics, the Transcaucasus, and Central Asia, as they have in Eastern Europe, particularly in Yugoslavia, where a civil war between the Serbs, the Croats, and the Bosnians has been tearing down that country. In China, on the other hand, the conflicts in Tibet and more recently in Xinjiang have given way to peaceful relations between the Han majority and more than fifty-five minority nationalities which live in various autonomous regions and provinces throughout the country.

Nationalism and national movements are phenomena that cannot be studied in isolation without taking into account the social and class structure of a society in which these movements arise. A class analysis of such movements, therefore, is imperative for a better understanding of the dynamics of social change. Class conflicts and class struggles are manifestations of social and political divisions in society that are at base a reflection of relations of production.[7] The specific nature of such production relations (i.e., class relations) come to inform the nature and content of the political struggles that at the *inter*-national level take the form of *national* struggles. Thus, while exploitative relations between two contending classes within a national boundary take the form of an internal class struggle, a similar relationship at the international level manifests itself in the form of a national struggle. This struggle, in essence, is the national expression of an international class struggle that is often based on an alliance of several classes unified for a single, immediate goal, national liberation.[8]

This process for self-determination, which is characteristic of Third World anti-imperialist national liberation struggles, is quite different in the advanced-capitalist imperial centers of Europe and North America. In these areas, the struggles waged by national minorities against the central state tend to be demands for limited autonomy, self-rule, or similar such status within the boundaries of the larger federal structure—demands that fall short of full national independence and statehood.[9]

In yet other instances, when the national question is raised within the context of a socialist state, we find an entirely different dynamic at work. In some cases, nationalities policy may be framed within the context of national integration, which at the same time recognizes cultural diversity and allows regional autonomy to various ethnic and nationality groups (as in China). In other cases, some national groups may come to play a disproportionately dominant role, where the center fails to deal with deep-seated national antagonisms inherited from an earlier period, which in time may give rise to the disintegration of the central state along national lines (as in the former Soviet Union). However, while long-suppressed national aspirations under an otherwise seemingly cooperative federated state may engender nationalism and national movements and *appear* to be "above class," it is important to stress that, here too, an analysis of the *class nature* of national movements is imperative for a clear understanding of the dynamics of such movements.

NATIONALISM, NATIONAL MOVEMENTS, AND CLASS STRUGGLE

A few key substantive questions that lie at the heart of nationalism must be briefly raised to sort out the class nature of a variety of national movements and struggles for national self-determination.[10] Thus, while all national movements possess characteristics that are historically specific, the central question that must be raised as theoretically applicable to all such struggles for national liberation is the necessity of a *class analysis approach* to the study of nationalism.

Nationalism, writes Albert Szymanski in his book *Class Structure*, "is the ideology that members of a nation, people, ethnic group, or 'racial' minority have more in common with each other than the various constituent classes of the group have with other people in similar class positions."[11] Moreover, "nationalism" dictates that because of their postulated overriding common interest, all classes within the ethnic group, people, or "racial" minority should work together economically and politically to advance their collective interests *against* other "nations," "races," ethnic groups, or peoples (even against those who are in the *same* classes). Nationalism is the advocacy of ethnic or "national" solidarity and action over class consciousness and action. It is, thus, the opposite of class consciousness that argues solidarity should occur and political alliances be formed primarily along *class* lines (even against the relatively privileged groups within one's subordinate ethnic group). Nationalism and class consciousness are, thus, alternative strategies of political action for gaining improvement in one's life.[12]

"In fact," adds Szymanski, "nationalism is a product of class forces. Although different kinds of nationalism differ qualitatively in their effects, *all* serve some classes within a given racial or ethnic group as opposed to others."[13]

The adoption of a *class analysis approach* to the study of nationalism, therefore, would entail an analysis of *the class base of a particular national movement, the balance of class forces within it, and the class forces leading the movement*. On this basis, one could determine the nature and future course of development of a national movement and whether a given movement is progressive or reactionary. Once the *class character* of a liberation movement and its leadership is thus determined, a political differentiation of various types of national movements can be ascertained, which in turn would provide us with clues to the social-political character of the movement in question.[14]

An understanding of the class nature of a given national movement may also inform us of the nature of the class forces that movement is struggling *against*, hence the nature and forms of the *class struggle*: the class content of the anti-imperialist liberation struggle transforms the national struggle into a *class* struggle which is fought out at the national and international levels; this struggle, which appears in the form of a national struggle, is, in essence, *a struggle for state power*.[15] "If national struggle . . . is class struggle, [i.e.,] . . . one very important form of the struggle for state power," writes James Blaut, then a number of questions arise that are central to an understanding of nationalism and a national movement: "which classes make use of it, in which historical epochs, and for which purposes?"[16] Thus, in this way, we can expect a relationship between the class character of a national movement, its political goals, and the nature and direction of the postindependence state following a successful national struggle.

NATIONALISM, CLASS STRUGGLE, AND SOCIAL TRANSFORMATION

National movements that are struggling for liberation are also engaged in struggles against dominant class forces that are in charge of the prevailing social order. As a result, national struggles for this very reason often turn into class struggles where a subordinate, oppressed class comes to express its interests through a revolutionary movement aimed at taking state power. In this sense, such a movement is often led by a single class or an alliance of class forces that have interests in opposition to those who control the state. Thus, a national movement led by the national or petty bourgeoisie, which can be characterized as "bourgeois nationalism," can, when it succeeds against imperialism, set the stage for the building of a national *capitalist* state. An anti-imperialist national movement led by the working class in alliance with the peasantry, on the other hand, can, upon waging a successful national liberation struggle, begin building a popular *socialist* state.[17]

In other instances, actions by a coalition of class forces that mobilizes a variety of social classes through cross-class alliances aimed at capturing state power may, due to the absence of a clearly articulated class position, result in the transformation of society in an ambiguous direction, such that in the absence of a clear and resolute action against existing social, political, and economic institutions of society, the new order may soon lose its dynamism and become incorporated into the structures of existing social arrangements. Given the dominating strength of imperialism in the world political economy, it is also important to recognize the force brought to bear by imperialism in shaping the nature and direction of such movements that have an immense impact on the balance of class forces at the global level. Such intervention by an external force becomes a crucial determinant of the class struggle when it is articulated through various internal class forces that are allied to it. An alliance of dominant classes at the global level is thus aimed at blocking the struggles of national movements in an effort to forestall the development of the class struggle that would transform the state and society and bring to power forces whose interests are contrary to and clash with those in control of the prevailing social order.

The critical factor that distinguishes the nature and dynamics of contemporary forms of nationalism and national movements, then, is the *class character* of these movements and their *class leadership*. It is within this context of social-political developments in the struggle against the existing state and social-economic structures of society that we begin to delineate the nature of the ongoing class struggles and social transformation embarked by movements for national liberation.

CONCLUSION

The diverse settings in which struggles for autonomy, self-determination, and national liberation take place necessitate a careful analysis of the relationship between class, nation, and state—phenomena that are central to our understanding of the nature and dynamics of nationalism, class struggle, and social transformation. It is thus within the framework of an understanding of the relationship between these phenomena that we find the social relevance of nationalism and national movements as manifested in different spatial, temporal, and political contexts. An analysis of the class nature of national movements, then, provides us a clear understanding of the nature, form, and class content of nationalism, as well as the nature and dynamics of the society that a given movement is struggling to build. With a clear class perspective on the ideology of nationalism and national movements, we can thus better comprehend this powerful and persistent phenomenon that has gripped the attention of the world community throughout the twentieth century.[18]

NOTES

1. For a detailed theoretical discussion on the rise of nationalism and national movements historically and today, see James M. Blaut, *The National Question: Decolonising the Theory of Nationalism* (London: Zed Books, 1987).

2. For an analysis of the internationalization of capital and its implications in the twentieth century, see Berch Berberoglu, *The Internationalization of Capital: Imperialism and Capitalist Development on a World Scale* (New York: Praeger, 1987).

3. See Eric Hobsbawm, *The Age of Revolution: 1789–1848* (New York: World, 1962), Chap. 7; and idem, *The Age of Capital: 1848–1875* (New York: Scribner's, 1975), Chap. 5.

4. For a discussion on the theory of nationalism and the various nationalist movements, see Horace B. Davis, *Toward a Marxist Theory of Nationalism* (New York: Monthly Review Press, 1978). See also Davis's earlier study, *Nationalism and Socialism: Marxist and Labor Theories of Nationalism to 1917* (New York: Monthly Review Press, 1967).

5. See Norman Miller and Roderick Aya, eds., *National Liberation: Revolution in the Third World* (New York: Free Press, 1971); Donald C. Hodges and Robert Elias Abu Shanab, eds., *NLF: National Liberation Fronts, 1960/1970* (New York: William Morrow & Co., 1972).

6. See B. J. Odeh, *Lebanon: Dynamics of Conflict* (London: Zed Press, 1985).

7. See Albert Szymanski, *Class Structure: A Critical Perspective* (New York: Praeger, 1983), pp. 5–7, 76–84.

8. James Blaut similarly argues that national liberation struggles against imperialism at the international level are, in essence, class struggles. See Blaut, *The National Question*, pp. 176–95.

9. This seems to be the case, for example, in Quebec and the Basque Provinces, as well as with the predicament of Native Americans in the United States and Canada.

10. For an extended analysis of various theoretical positions and debates on the theory of nationalism and the national question, see Blaut, *The National Question*, esp. Chap. 1.

11. Szymanski, *Class Structure*, p. 430.

12. Ibid.

13. Ibid.

14. See Berberoglu, *The Internationalization of Capital*, Chap. 7. See also Berch Berberoglu, *Political Sociology: A Comparative/Historical Approach* (New York: General Hall, 1990), Chap. 2.

15. Ibid. See also Blaut, *The National Question*, pp. 23, 46, 123.

16. Blaut, *The National Question*, pp. 4, 46.

17. Albert Szymanski, *The Logic of Imperialism* (New York: Praeger, 1981), pp. 426–29, 537.

18. For case studies of nationalism and national movements throughout the twentieth century, including those in Palestine, Kurdistan, South Africa, Puerto Rico, Northern Ireland, the Basque Country, Quebec, the former Soviet Union, China, and Yugoslavia, see Berch Berberoglu (ed.), *The National Question: Nationalism, Ethnic Conflict, and Self-Determination* (Philadelphia: Temple University Press, 1994).

Seven

Class, Race, and Gender

The exploitation of labor for private profit is a central characteristic of capitalism and capitalist societies around the world. This exploitation is further facilitated by capital and the capitalist state through various means—especially through racial and gender oppression. Although patriarchy and racial oppression have existed long before the emergence of capitalism, capitalist society has historically incorporated these two forms of oppression into its mode of capital accumulation since the sixteenth century. The differential exploitation of the working class through its division along racial and gender lines has thus become a source of greater profit (and control) at the expense of the working class and has been (and continues to be) an important impediment to the full-scale development of class consciousness among workers to overcome capitalist domination.

This chapter examines the class nature of racial and gender oppression under capitalism and provides an analysis of the processes by which capital has secured for itself a racially and sexually differentiated working class that it can exploit to further the accumulation of capital. The relationship between class, race, and gender are thus examined in the context of the processes that facilitate the control and exploitation of labor within capitalist society.

CLASS, RACE, AND EXPLOITATION

The origins of racial oppression in the modern world go back to colonialism and the slave trade. The colonial expansion of Europe during the sixteenth through the eighteenth centuries and the consequent "turning of

Africa into a warren for the commercial hunting of black-skins"[1] facilitated the development of capitalism in Europe and later the United States.

"With the new world," writes the great African-American scholar W. E. B. Du Bois, "came fatally the African slave trade and Negro slavery in the Americas":

There were new cruelties, new hatreds of human beings, and new degradations of human labor. The temptation to degrade human labor was made vaster and deeper by the incredible accumulation of wealth based on slave labor.[2]

"U.S. capitalists, starting in the colonial period," writes political economist Victor Perlo, "were major participants in this cruel and inhuman process of self-enrichment."[3] The slave system that was established in the U.S. South during the colonial era shaped the contours of life in the United States for many decades. "It was the southern slave owners," Perlo adds, "who, for the first 80 years of U.S. independence, were major garners of wealth through the forced labor of these slaves and their children and grandchildren."[4] The cruel treatment of slaves by the white master class and society in general turned them into a mere commodity to be exploited for the maximization of profit for the owners. "These slaves," Du Bois observes, "could be bought and sold, could move from place to place only with permission, were forbidden to learn to read or write, legally could never hold property or marry."[5]

After the defeat of the South in the Civil War and the brief period of Reconstruction, the plantations were restored to the former slave owners and a system of sharecropping, accompanied by segregation, was imposed on black people. In time, the ex-slaves became farm laborers, and then industrial workers in the mines and mills of modern capital as wage labor. Thus, during the century following emancipation, more and more blacks became part of an expanding working class, and the black community in general began to undergo internal social differentiation such that a more complex class structure began to develop among blacks in the United States.

The changing dynamics of the developing class structure in the African American community prompted black intellectuals to take up a closer examination of the relationship between race and class, as the intersection of these two phenomena took on new meaning in addressing the problems of class, race, and exploitation in contemporary U.S. society.

Aware of the development of classes within the African American community in the United States, Du Bois, in the latter part of his life, forcefully argued that as current trends in capitalist expansion in America encroach on the African American community, they too will find themselves engaged in class conflict and class struggle, for it is in the nature of capitalism itself that contradictions along class lines develop and mature in the direction of a struggle between the chief antagonistic classes, and the African American community is not exempt from this fundamental law of capitalist expansion. Thus:

The main danger and the central question of the capitalistic development through which the Negro-American group is forced to go is the question of the ultimate control of the capital which they must raise and use. If this capital is going to be controlled by a few men for their own benefit, then we are destined to suffer from our own capitalists exactly what we are suffering from white capitalists today.[6]

Speaking of "inner class division based on income and exploitation," Du Bois argued that by the middle of the twentieth century "it was clear that the great machine of big business was sweeping not only the mass of white Americans . . . it had also and quite naturally swept Negroes into the same maelstrom."[7] He went on to point out that, with the fall of official segregation in public accommodations and schools, blacks "will be divided into classes even more sharply than now."[8]

Adopting more and more a class analysis approach to the race question, Du Bois during the latter years of his life began to develop "firm and decided views about the basis for race discrimination" in class terms: "He continually pointed to the wage differential between black and white workers as the material basis for racism."[9]

E. Franklin Frazier was another prominent black intellectual who provided an equally penetrating analysis of the interconnection of race and class in the United States. Going beyond his earlier studies of race relations and the black family, Frazier's views on racism later became more and more informed by class analysis.[10] "Influenced by the class-based theories of left intellectuals and organizations," writes Anthony Platt, "by the 1930s . . . [Frazier's] writings tended to reinterpret the history of race relations through a prism of exploitation."[11]

"The introduction of the Negro into America," Frazier pointed out, "was due to the economic expansion of Europe" and that "the fate of Negro slavery was determined by economic forces"; in this sense, "the Negro's status in the United States," he stressed, "has been bound up, in the final analysis, with the role which the Negro has played in the economic system."[12] Framing the problem in such broader, historical, and structural terms, Frazier, Platt points out, "located the fundamental roots of racism in the dynamics of class relations on a global scale."[13]

Both Du Bois and Frazier understood racism as a manifestation of class conflict. They understood, therefore, that social emancipation would be the outcome of a resolution of the struggle between the main opposing classes in society. Although Du Bois's views on the forms the struggle would take differed from Frazier's, both agreed on the necessity of social change to end exploitation and thus facilitate the development of peaceful relations between the races.

Whereas Du Bois argued in favor of gradual transformation of societal institutions to combat racism through progressive political reforms, Frazier saw no other viable alternative to resolve the race question except through a radical transformation of the existing social-economic system. Much more forceful and direct, Frazier argued that there could be "no fundamental changes in race relations . . . unless these changes are brought about in connection with some revolutionary movement": However well intentioned, "the accumulation of goodwill will not do it," he added, because "the present racial situation is bound up with the present economic and social system."[14]

While the changing class composition of the African-American community in more recent decades gave rise to the subsequent debate on the caste and class controversy between William Julius Wilson, Charles Willie, and others in a different context,[15] Frazier's anticipation of the development of a new dynamic through the evolving contradictions of capitalist society in the late twentieth century led him to optimistic conclusions on the possibility of black-white unity within the working class, targeting the capitalists as the source of racial oppression and class exploitation of an increasingly integrated multiracial and multinational working class. Drawing his optimism on this point from the effects of the Great Depression on labor in the 1930s, and observing the "spread of radical ideas among working class Negroes through cooperation with white workers,"[16] Frazier projected that "as the Negro may become an integral part of the proletariat, . . . the feeling against his color may break down in the face of a common foe."[17] Clarifying his position on the interplay of race, class, and social emancipation, "In the urban environment," he wrote, the black worker "is showing signs of understanding the struggle for power between the proletariat and the owning classes, and is beginning to cooperate with white workers in this struggle which offers the only hope of his complete emancipation."[18] Thus, with the development of proletarian class consciousness, the black workers would come to merge with other sections of the working class and thereby identify their cause as one that is opposed to the class rule of capital.

CLASS, GENDER, AND PATRIARCHY

Historically, patriarchy and the oppression of women in society coincided with the development of social classes and class struggles. The transformation of the status of the female sex from a central component of primitive society to one subordinated to male domination through patriarchal social relations was the result of the emergence of class domination and exploitation in general.

Throughout history, from slavery to feudalism to capitalism, the oppression of women continued to constitute an important part of the exploitation and oppression of labor in class-divided societies. In time, the subordination of women to men became consolidated as part of the social landscape complementing the overall exploitation of the laboring people that the masses came to suffer in class society.

Capitalism and capitalist relations of production that became established in the eighteenth century further facilitated the oppression of women through cheap labor and domestic work to advance the interests of the capitalist class in the process of expanded capital accumulation.

The recognition of the interconnection between gender and class as part of the process of development of the family, private property, and inheritance was forcefully made by Frederick Engels, who understood the role of production relations in shaping the broader social relations of class society.[19] Decades later, another champion of the working class and of women's rights, Alexandra Kollontai, took up the task of exposing the root causes of women's oppression and showed the way for the emancipation of women in capitalist society.

"The conditions and forms of production," Kollontai wrote in *The Social Basis of the Woman Question*, "have subjugated women throughout human history, and have gradually relegated them to the position of oppression and dependence in which most of them existed until now."[20] Kollontai argued that since "specific economic factors were behind the subordination of women . . . a colossal upheaval of the entire social and economic structure was required before women could begin to retrieve the significance and independence they had lost."[21]

In another essay titled "Sexual Relations and the Class Struggle," Kollontai writes, "every new class that develops as a result of an advance in economic growth and material culture offers an appropriately new ideology. The code of sexual behavior is part of this ideology."[22] "All the experience of history teaches us," she concludes, "that a social group works out its ideology, consequently its sexual morality, in the process of its struggle with hostile social forces"[23]—forces which constitute the very basis of class struggle in society.

Kollontai's analysis of the nature and sources of women's oppression led her to look for a class solution to the emancipation of women. The rights of women, she argued, could not be achieved while society was organized on the basis of private profit. Going beyond the critique of capitalism and the exploitation of labor in general, Kollontai placed the interests of women workers at the forefront of her analysis and examined the struggles of working women and their families in late nineteenth-century capitalist society, which preceded the bourgeois women's movement that emerged later during this period, bringing into sharp focus the class content of women's rights under capitalism.

Providing a class analysis approach to the study of women's position in capitalist society, Kollontai, like Rosa Luxemburg and Clara Zetkin, defined the rights and interests of women on the basis of their *class* position, not their gender alone. She developed a sharp critique of the feminist movement for representing the interests of only a segment of the female population—bourgeois women. Siding with the working class politically and advocating the transformation of capitalist society, Kollontai focused her attention on working women and saw their liberation as part of the process of emancipation of the working class from capitalist exploitation.

The class essence of women's rights, as manifested in the position of women in society with respect to labor, is clearly driven home in Kollontai's works where she focuses on the problems of working women as they occur in their daily material life conditions. The exploitation of working women thus takes on a special, *class* meaning, as Kollontai differentiates the experiences (and thereby the interests) of women of different classes—a distinction which has important political implications.

In pointing to the intricate relationship of class and gender in capitalist society, and the necessity of the struggle against women's oppression, Kollontai argues that one must fight for the "fundamental transformation of the contemporary economic and social structure of society without which the liberation of women cannot be complete."[24] This means that, to put an end to the oppression of women, a major transformation of the existing capitalist order must take place—one that requires a revolutionary restructuring of social, economic, and political life that characterizes the fundamental structures of capitalist society. Kollontai asks, "Can political equality in the context of the retention of the entire capitalist-exploiter system free the working woman from that abyss of evil and suffering which pursues and oppresses her both as a woman and as a human being?"[25] And she answers it as follows:

The more aware among proletarian women realize that neither political nor juridical equality can solve the women's question in all its aspects. While women are compelled to sell their labor power and bear the yoke of capitalism, while the present exploitative system of producing new values continues to exist, they cannot become free and independent persons.[26]

Thus, the aim of the women workers, Kollontai points out, "is to abolish all privileges deriving from birth or wealth" and that, therefore, they are in this sense "fighting for the common class cause, while at the same time outlining and putting forward those needs and demands that most nearly affect themselves as women, housewives and mothers."[27] The struggles of working women, therefore, "are part and parcel of the common workers' cause!"[28]

There was a time when working men thought that they alone must bear on their shoulders the brunt of the struggle against capital, that they alone must deal with the "old world" without the help of their womenfolk. However, as working-class women entered the labor market by need, by the fact that husband or father is unemployed, working men became aware that to leave women behind in the ranks of the "non-class-conscious" was to damage their cause and hold it back. The greater the number of conscious fighters, the greater the chances of success. . . .

Every special, distinct form of work among the women of the working class is simply a means of arousing the consciousness of the woman worker and drawing her into the ranks of those fighting for a better future. . . . [The] meticulous work undertaken to arouse the self-consciousness of the woman worker are serving the cause . . . of the unification of the working class.[29]

It is in this context of the broader interests of the working class as a whole that Kollontai developed her understanding of the interplay between class, gender, and patriarchy, and identified the centrality of the exploitation of labor for private profit as the basis of the oppression and exploitation of working women in capitalist society.

The necessity of the struggle against women's oppression simultaneously with the struggle against capitalist exploitation has been further developed by Marxist feminists in recent decades. Providing an in-depth analysis of the intersection of class and gender in capitalist society, Marxist feminists have made an important contribution to a clear, class-based understanding of the causes and consequences of women's oppression under capitalism.

CONCLUSION

Patriarchy and racial oppression, which developed with the emergence of class divisions in society, have become the twin pillars of capital accumulation through the exploitation of labor in capitalist society. Facilitating the accumulation process to generate greater profits for the capitalists, racial and gender oppression have thus become part of the process of capitalist development to maintain the system and to secure its future. Thus, racial and gender divisions have come to serve more than the greater profit needs of capital through pay differentials; they have provided capital with the weapon of "divide and rule" to maintain its power over society and to assure its continued control of the state and other vital social institutions that secure the class rule of the capitalist class.

A class analysis of racial and gender oppression is imperative for a clear understanding of the connection of these phenomena with the broader exploitation of labor to maximize profits for the capitalists—an exploitation that is especially severe and more cruel when it is directed against women workers and workers of racial and ethnic minorities. The class essence of racial and gender oppression becomes apparent when we examine the class nature of capital's behavior toward women and minorities. Thus, as Kollontai and Frazier have pointed out, while a small segment of these populations can escape this oppression and become beneficiaries of capitalist rule, the working people in general, and women and minority workers in particular, are the clear victims of capitalist exploitation that capital has come to understand as something beneficial for its continued accumulation of wealth and rule over society.

NOTES

1. Karl Marx, *Capital*, Vol. I (New York: International Publishers, 1967), p. 751.

2. W.E.B. Du Bois, "The White Masters of the World," in Virginia Hamilton (ed.), *The Writings of W.E.B. Du Bois* (New York: Thomas Y. Crowell Company, 1975), pp. 201–202.

3. Victor Perlo, *Super Profits and Crises: Modern U.S. Capitalism* (New York: International Publishers, 1988), p. 85.

4. Ibid.

5. W.E.B. Du Bois, "The Social Effects of Emancipation," in Meyer Weinberg (ed.), *W.E.B. Du Bois: A Reader* (New York: Harper & Row, 1970), p. 71.

6. Ibid., pp. 342–43.

7. Du Bois, quoted in Gerald Horne, *Black & Red: W.E.B. Du Bois and the Afro-American Response to the Cold War, 1944–1963* (Albany: State University of New York Press, 1986), p. 224.

8. W.E.B. Du Bois, "Negroes and the Crisis of Capitalism in the United States," *Monthly Review* 4, no. 12 (April 1953), pp. 482–483.

9. Horne, *Black & Red*, p. 225.

10. For his earlier studies, see, for example, E. Franklin Frazier, *The Negro Family in the United States* (Chicago: University of Chicago Press, 1939). His later views on the relationship of race and class are developed in E. Franklin Frazier, *The Negro in the United States* (New York: Macmillan, 1949); and idem, *Race and Culture Contacts in the Modern World* (New York: Knopf, 1957).

11. Anthony M. Platt, *E. Franklin Frazier Reconsidered* (New Brunswick, NJ: Rutgers University Press, 1991), p. 164.

12. Frazier, quoted in Platt, *E. Franklin Frazier Reconsidered*, p. 164.

13. Ibid., p. 219.

14. Frazier, quoted in Platt, *E. Franklin Frazier Reconsidered*, p. 186.

15. This controversy, which began with the publication of William Julius Wilson's *The Declining Significance of Race* (Chicago: University of Chicago Press, 1978) and continued through his *The Truly Disadvantaged: The Inner City, the Underclass, and Public Policy* (Chicago: University of Chicago Press, 1987), took place within the context of the changing dynamics of the class structure within the black community resulting from the transformation of the U.S. economy and its impact on urban centers, which gave rise to an "underclass" of largely unemployed or menially employed black population trapped in America's central cities. For an overview of the different positions taken in this debate, see, for example, Charles V. Willie (ed.), *The Caste and Class Controversy on Race and Poverty* (Dix Hills, N.Y.: General Hall, 1989).

16. Frazier, quoted in Platt, *E. Franklin Frazier Reconsidered*, p. 164.

17. Ibid., p. 163.

18. Ibid., p. 164.

19. Frederick Engels, *The Origin of the Family, Private Property and the State* (New York: International Publishers, 1972).

20. Alexandra Kollontai, "The Social Basis of the Woman Question" in Alix Holt (ed.), *Selected Writings of Alexandra Kollontai* (Westport, Conn.: Lawrence Hill and Company, 1978), p. 61.

21. Ibid., pp. 58, 61.

22. Alexandra Kollontai, "Sexual Relations and the Class Struggle," in Holt, *Selected Writings of Alexandra Kollontai*, p. 249.

23. Ibid.

24. Ibid., pp. 59–60.

25. Kollontai, in I. M. Dazhina et al., (eds.), *Alexandra Kollontai: Selected Articles and Speeches* (New York: International Publishers, 1984), pp. 33–34.

26. Ibid., p. 34.

27. Ibid., p. 64.

28. Ibid.

29. Ibid., pp. 62–65. Addressing the hopes and aspirations of millions of working women, Kollontai proclaimed: "Let a joyous sense of serving the common class cause and of fighting simultaneously for their own female emancipation inspire women workers to join in the celebration,"p. 65.

Conclusion

I have in this book examined various aspects of social classes and class structure in comparative historical perspective. The theoretical issues raised regarding the nature of classes and class inequality have provided the intellectual raw materials for an analysis of the class structure of concrete societies in which class relations take place. Adopting the historical materialist approach to the study of class structure and class struggle in historically specific social formations defined by a dominant mode of production, I have examined the nature and dynamics of various forms of class systems historically and across territorial boundaries. Through this study of a multiplicity of class configurations and productive relations over centuries of human social development in different historical and geographic settings, I have reached the following conclusions on the nature and dynamics of class relations in society at the broader macrosociological level.

First, it is evident from the many anthropological studies that have investigated the origins of social classes and class inequality that the exploitation of one class by another did not exist for tens of thousands of years, for most of human history. Class exploitation is a recent phenomenon that emerged with the rise of a social surplus. This, in turn, led to internal social strife and the formation of classes through the instrumentality of a state that came to constitute the first great empires of antiquity.

Second, with the emergence of social classes and the consolidation of privilege on a private basis in late despotic, slave-owning, feudal, and capitalist societies, there ensued a struggle between the main class forces in society engaged in relations of production that generate material wealth. The unequal distribution of this wealth between the laboring masses and the owners of the means of production thus led to class struggle over the distribution of that wealth and control of the state, the superstructural institution that serves to legitimize and protect the interests of the dominant ruling class in society.

Third, as class exploitation and class conflict developed and matured over the centuries, the ensuing class struggle between the chief contending classes in society became the motive force of social transformation that led to the overthrow of one system after another. The transformation of primitive communal to despotic to slave-owning to feudal to capitalist modes of production came to be characterized as the historical process of development of class systems, with class struggle as the motive force of social transformation.

Fourth, through an analysis of the class structure of different historically specific societies defined by their dominant mode of production, I have demonstrated the similarities and differences between a diverse set of class structures prevalent in varied class systems. Focusing on the class structure of capitalist societies, I have shown that the inner logic of class relations and class struggles under capitalism is based on the exploitation of labor for private profit and that this process lies at the heart of the class struggles that have developed over the past two centuries where capitalist relations of production have made major inroads. The class struggles that are now taking place throughout the capitalist world are thus the direct result of the internationalization of capital and capitalist relations of production that have spread to many corners of the world over the course of the twentieth century.

Finally, as a direct outgrowth of the processes examined throughout this book, I have argued that race, ethnic, and gender relations are essential components of class structure that have a major impact on class relations and class struggles. Through a detailed analysis of the social basis of racism, nationalism, and patriarchy, I have argued that to develop a proper understanding of these phenomena, we must examine the class nature of their dynamics and situate them within the broader context of class analysis.

Clearly, given the history of domination and exploitation of one class by another in successive forms of class society, the transformation of social relations at the societal level cannot take place without a thorough transformation of the existing class structure, and the overthrow of the old order and the emergence of a new one depend on the degree of success of the class forces struggling to effect change in a new, progressive direction.

Through an analysis of a multiplicity of theoretical and empirical issues, I have in this book attempted to address the question of class and its nature and dynamics in historical and macrosociological perspective. Adopting the historical materialist approach to explain the process of social change and social development through time and in different societal settings, I have attempted to provide a comprehensive yet concise analysis of class structure and social transformation. This book has asked the kinds of questions that make the study of class structure a rewarding intellectual experience, questions, I hope, that will facilitate a further and more detailed analysis of the most decisive phenomenon of our time—*class*.

Bibliography

Alavi, Hamza. 1982. "State and Class under Peripheral Capitalism," in H. Alavi and T. Shanin (eds.), *An Introduction to the Sociology of "Developing Societies."* London: Macmillan.

Alexander, I. 1987. "Real Wages and Class Struggle in South Korea." *Journal of Contemporary Asia* 17, no. 4.

Althusser, Louis. 1969. *For Marx.* London: Penguin.

_____. 1971. *Lenin and Philosophy and Other Essays.* London: New Left Books.

_____. 1976. *Essays in Self-Criticism.* London: New Left Books.

Althusser, Louis, and Etienne Balibar. 1968. *Reading Capital.* London: New Left Books.

Amara, Hamid Ait, and Bernard Founou-Tchuigoua (eds.). 1990. *African Agriculture: The Critical Choices.* London: Zed Books.

Amin, Samir. 1976. *Unequal Development: An Essay on the Social Formations of Peripheral Capitalism.* New York: Monthly Review Press.

_____. 1978. *The Arab Nation: Nationalism and Class Struggles.* London: Zed Press.

Anderson, Charles H. 1974. *The Political Economy of Social Class.* Englewood Cliffs, N.J.: Prentice-Hall.

Anderson, P. 1974. *Lineages of the Absolutist State.* London: New Left Books.

_____. 1974. *Passages from Antiquity to Feudalism.* London: New Left Books.

Andreski, Stanislav. 1968. *Military Organization and Society.* Berkeley: University of California Press.

Aptheker, Herbert. 1960. *The American Revolution, 1763–1783.* New York: International Publishers.

_____. 1960. *The World of C. Wright Mills.* New York: Marzani and Munsell.

_____. 1973. *Annotated Bibliography of the Published Writings of W.E.B. Du Bois.* Millwood, N.Y.: Kraus-Thomson Organization Ltd.

_____. 1976. *Early Years of the Republic.* New York: International Publishers.

Aronowitz, Stanley. 1973. *False Promises: The Shaping of American Working-Class Consciousness*. New York: McGraw-Hill.

———. 1983. *Working Class Hero: A New Strategy for Labor*. New York: Adama Books.

Ayala, Cesar J. 1989. "Theories of Big Business in American Society." *Critical Sociology* 16, no. 2–3 (Summer-Fall).

Babu, Abdul Rahman Mohamed. 1981. *African Socialism or Socialist Africa?* London: Zed Press.

Baker, Elizabeth Faulkner. 1964. *Technology and Women's Work*. New York: Columbia University Press.

Balibar, Etienne. 1977. *On the Dictatorship of the Proletariat*. London: New Left Books.

Baran, Paul, and Paul M. Sweezy. 1966. *Monopoly Capital*. New York: Monthly Review Press.

Batatu, Hanna. 1978. *The Old Social Classes and the Revolutionary Movements of Iraq*. Princeton: Princeton University Press.

Beard, Charles. 1962. *An Economic Interpretation of the Constitution of the United States*. New York: Macmillan.

Beard, Charles, and Mary Beard. 1930. *The Rise of American Civilization*. New York: Macmillan.

Beechey, Veronica, and Tessa Perkins. 1987. *A Matter of Hours: Women, Part-time Work, and the Labor Market*. Minneapolis: University of Minnesota Press.

Beinin, Joel. 1982. "Egypt's Transition Under Nasser." *MERIP Reports*, no. 107 (July-August).

Bello, Walden, and Stephanie Rosenfeld. 1990. *Dragons in Distress: Conflict in Asia's Miracle Economies*. San Francisco: Institute for Food and Development Policy.

Belov, Gennady. 1986. *What Is the State?* Moscow: Progress Publishers.

Beneria, Lourdes. 1989. "Gender and the Global Economy." In Arthur MacEwan and William K. Tabb (eds.), *Instability and Change in the World Economy*. New York: Monthly Review Press.

Berberoglu, Berch. 1977. "The Transition from Feudalism to Capitalism: The Sweezy-Dobb Debate." *Revista Mexicana de Sociologia* 39, no. 4 (October-December).

———. 1980. "The Nature and Contradictions of State Capitalism in the Third World." *Social and Economic Studies* 28, no. 2.

———. 1980. "Pre-Capitalist Modes of Production: Their Origins, Contradictions, and Transformation." *Quarterly Review of Historical Studies* 19, nos. 1–2.

———. 1986. *India: National Liberation and Class Struggles*. Meerut, India: Sarup & Sons.

———. 1987. "The Contradictions of Export-Oriented Development in the Third World." *Social and Economic Studies* 36, no. 4 (December).

———. 1987. *The Internationalization of Capital: Imperialism and Capitalist Development on a World Scale*. New York: Praeger.

———. 1989. *Power and Stability in the Middle East*. London: Zed Books.

———. 1990. *Political Sociology: A Comparative/Historical Approach*. New York: General Hall.

———. 1992. *Class, State and Development in India*. New Delhi: Sage Publications.

———. 1992. *The Legacy of Empire: Economic Decline and Class Polarization in the United States*. New York: Praeger.

———. 1992. *The Political Economy of Development: Development Theory and the Prospects for Change in the Third World*. Albany: State University of New York Press.

———. 1993. *An Introduction to Classical and Contemporary Social Theory: A Critical Perspective*. New York: General Hall.

———. 1993. *The Labor Process and Control of Labor: The Changing Nature of Work Relations in the Late Twentieth Century*. New York: Praeger.

———. 1994. *The National Question: Nationalism, Ethnic Conflict, and Self-Determination*. Philadelphia: Temple University Press.

Bettelheim, Charles. 1976. *Class Struggles in the USSR: First Period, 1917–1923*. New York: Monthly Review Press.

———. 1978. *Class Struggles in the USSR: Second Period, 1923–1930*. New York: Monthly Review Press.

Bina, Cyrus, and Behzad Yaghmaian. 1991. "Post-War Global Accumulation and the Transnationalization of Capital." *Capital & Class*, no. 43 (Spring).

Biro, Lajos, and Marc J. Cohen, eds. 1979. *The United States in Crisis*. Minneapolis: MEP Press.

Blanco, Hugo. 1972. *Land or Death: The Peasant Struggle in Peru*. New York: Pathfinder Press.

Blau, Francine D. 1984. "Women in the Labor Force: An Overview," in Joe Freeman (ed.), *Women: A Feminist Perspective*. Palo Alto, Calif.: Mayfield.

Blaut, James M. 1987. *The National Question: Decolonising the Theory of Nationalism*. London: Zed Books.

Block, Fred. 1977. "The Ruling Class Does Not Rule: Notes on the Marxist Theory of the State." *Socialist Review*, no. 33 (May–June).

———. 1978. "Class Consciousness and Capitalist Rationalization: A Reply to Critics." *Socialist Review*, nos. 40–41 (July–October).

———. 1987. *Revising State Theory*. Philadelphia: Temple University Press.

Bluestone, Barry, and Bennett Harrison. 1982. *The Deindustrialization of America*. New York: Basic Books.

Bollinger, William. 1977. "The Bourgeois Revolution in Peru." *Latin American Perspectives* 4, no. 3 (Summer).

Bottomore, Tom, and Robert J. Brym, eds. 1989. *The Capitalist Class: An International Study*. New York: New York University Press.

Bowles, Samuel, and Richard Edwards. 1985. *Understanding Capitalism*. New York: Harper & Row.

Boyer, Richard, and Herbert Morais. 1980. *Labor's Untold Story*. 3rd ed. New York: United Electrical, Radio, and Machine Workers of America.

Braun, Denny. 1991. *The Rich Get Richer: The Rise of Income Inequality in the United States and the World*. Chicago: Nelson-Hall Publishers.

Braverman, Harry. 1974. *Labor and Monopoly Capital: The Degradation of Work in the Twentieth Century*. New York: Monthly Review Press.

Brecher, Jeremy. 1972. *Strike!* Greenwich, Conn.: Fawcet.

Brenner, Robert. 1977. "The Origins of Capitalist Development: A Critique of Neo-Smithian Marxism." *New Left Review*, no. 104 (July-August).

Burris, Val. 1987. "Class Structure and Political Ideology." *Critical Sociology* 14, no. 2 (Summer).

_____. 1988. "New Directions in Class Analysis." *Critical Sociology* 15, no. 1 (Spring).

Callinicos, Alex. 1989. *Against Postmodernism: A Marxist Critique*. New York: St. Martin's Press.

Calvert, Peter. 1982. *The Concept of Class*. New York: St. Martin's Press.

Cameron, Kenneth Neill. 1977. *Humanity and Society: A World History*. New York: Monthly Review Press.

Carchedi, Guglielmo. 1977. *The Economic Identification of Social Classes*. London: Routledge & Kegan Paul.

_____. 1986. "Two Models of Class Analysis." *Capital and Class* 29.

Carnoy, Martin. 1984. *The State and Political Theory*. Princeton: Princeton University Press.

Chaliand, Gerard, ed. 1980. *People Without a Country: The Kurds and Kurdistan*. London: Zed Press.

Chaliand, Gerard, and Yves Ternon. 1983. *The Armenians: From Genocide to Resistance*. London: Zed Press.

Chandra, Bipan. 1975. "The Indian Capitalist Class and Imperialism Before 1947." *Journal of Contemporary Asia* 5, no. 3.

Chattopadhyay, Paresh. 1992. "India's Capitalist Industrialization," in Berch Berberoglu (ed.), *Class, State, and Development in India*. New Delhi: Sage Publications.

Cheru, Fantu. 1989. *The Silent Revolution in Africa: Debt, Development and Democracy*. London: Zed Books.

Chilcote, Ronald H., ed. 1982. *Dependency and Marxism: Toward a Resolution of the Debate*. Boulder, Colo.: Westview Press.

Childe, V. Gordon. 1971. *What Happened in History*. Baltimore: Penguin.

Clapham, John. 1948. *The Economic Development of France and Germany*. Cambridge: Cambridge University Press.

Clarke, S. 1977. "Marxism, Sociology and Poulantzas's Theory of the State." *Capital and Class* 2.

Clawson, Patrick. 1977. "The Internationalization of Capital and Capital Accumulation in Iran and Iraq." *Insurgent Sociologist* 7, no. 2 (Spring).

Cockcroft, James D. 1986. *Outlaws in the Promised Land: Mexican Immigrant Workers and America's Future*. New York: Grove Press.

Cooper, Mark. 1983. "Egyptian State Capitalism in Crisis," in Talal Asad and Roger Owen (eds.), *The Middle East*. New York: Monthly Review Press.

Coulson, Andrew. 1982. *Tanzania: A Political Economy*. Oxford: Clarendon Press.

Crompton, Rosemary, and Jon Gubbay. 1978. *Economy and Class Structure*. New York: St. Martin's Press.

Cypher, James. 1979. "The Internationalization of Capital and the Transformation of Social Formations: A Critique of the Monthly Review School." *Review of Radical Political Economics* 11, no. 4.

Dahrendorf, Ralph. 1959. *Class and Class Conflict in Industrial Society*. Stanford: Stanford University Press.

Davidson, Basil. 1961. *The African Slave Trade*. Boston: Little, Brown.

Davis, Horace B. 1967. *Nationalism and Socialism: Marxist and Labor Theories of Nationalism to 1917.* New York: Monthly Review Press.

———. 1978. *Toward a Marxist Theory of Nationalism.* New York: Monthly Review Press.

Davis, Kingsley, and Wilbert E. Moore. 1945. "Some Principles of Stratification." *American Sociological Review* 10, no. 2 (April).

Davis, Mike. 1986. *Prisoners of the American Dream: Politics and Economy in the History of the U.S. Working Class.* London: Verso.

Dazhina, I. M., et al., eds. 1984. *Alexandra Kollontai: Selected Articles and Speeches.* New York: International Publishers.

De Caux, Len. 1970. *Labor Radical.* Boston: Beacon Press.

Deegan, Mary Jo, ed. 1991. *Women in Sociology.* Westport, Conn.: Greenwood Press.

Desai, A. R. 1984. *India's Path of Development.* Bombay: Popular Prakashan.

Devine, Jim. 1982. "The Structural Crisis of U.S. Capitalism." *Southwest Economy and Society* 6, no. 1 (Fall).

Deyo, Frederick, Stephen Heggard, and Hagen Koo. 1987. "Labor in the Political Economy of East Asian Industrialization." *Bulletin of Concerned Asian Scholars* 19, no. 2.

Domhoff, G. William. 1967. *Who Rules America?* Englewood Cliffs, N.J.: Prentice-Hall.

———. 1971. *The Higher Circles: The Governing Class in America.* New York: Vintage.

———. 1978. *The Powers That Be: Processes of Ruling Class Domination in America.* New York: Vintage.

———. 1990. *The Power Elite and the State.* New York: Aldine de Gruyter.

Dore, Elizabeth, and John Weeks. 1976. "The Intensification of the Assault Against the Working Class in 'Revolutionary' Peru." *Latin American Perspectives* 3, no. 2 (Spring).

———. 1977. "Class Alliances and Class Struggle in Peru." *Latin American Perspectives* 4, no. 3 (Summer).

Dowd, Douglas F. 1977. *The Twisted Dream: Capitalist Development in the United States Since 1776.* Cambridge, Mass.: Winthrop.

Draper, Hal. 1977. *Karl Marx's Theory of Revolution: State and Bureaucracy.* Parts 1 and 2. New York: Monthly Review Press.

Du Bois, W.E.B. 1953. "Negroes and the Crisis of Capitalism in the United States." *Monthly Review* 4, no. 12 (April).

———. 1970. "The Social Effects of Emancipation." and "The Class Struggle," in Meyer Weinberg (ed.), *W.E.B. Du Bois: A Reader.* New York: Harper & Row.

———. 1975. "The White Masters of the World," in Virginia Hamilton (ed.), *The Writings of W.E.B. Du Bois.* New York: Thomas Y. Crowell Company.

Dunne, John G. 1967. *Delano, The Story of the California Grape Strike.* New York: Farrar, Straus & Giroux.

Durkheim, Emile. 1964. *The Division of Labor in Society.* New York: Free Press.

Elison, Diane, and Ruth Pearson. 1981. "Nimble Fingers Make Cheap Workers: An Analysis of Workers in Employment in Third World Export Processing." *Feminist Review* 33.

Engels, Frederick. 1972. *The Origin of the Family, Private Property and the State.* New York: International Publishers.

_____ . 1973. *The Peasant War in Germany.* New York: International Publishers.

_____ . 1976. *Anti-Duhring.* New York: International Publishers.

Erickson, Gerald, and Harold L. Schwartz, eds. 1977. *Social Class in the Contemporary United States.* Minneapolis: Marxist Educational Press.

Esping-Andersen, Gosta, Roger Friedland, and Erik Olin Wright. 1976. "Modes of Class Struggle and the Capitalist State." *Kapitalistate,* nos. 4–5 (Summer).

Fantasia, Rick. 1988. *Cultures of Solidarity: Consciousness, Action, and Contemporary American Workers.* Berkeley: University of California Press.

Farsoun, Karen. 1975. "State Capitalism in Algeria." *MERIP Reports,* no. 35.

Fernandez, Raul, and Jose F. Ocampo. 1974. "The Latin American Revolution: A Theory of Imperialism, Not Dependence." *Latin American Perspectives* 1, no. 1 (Spring).

Fiori, Giuseppe. 1970. *Antonio Gramsci, Life of a Revolutionary.* London: New Left Books.

Fitzgerald, E.V.K. 1979. *The Political Economy of Peru, 1956–78.* Cambridge: Cambridge University Press.

Foster, John. 1974. *Class Struggle and the Industrial Revolution.* New York: St. Martin's Press.

_____ . 1986. *The Theory of Monopoly Capitalism.* New York: Monthly Review Press.

Foster, John Bellamy, and Henryk Szlajfer, eds. 1984. *The Faltering Economy: The Problem of Accumulation Under Monopoly Capitalism.* New York: Monthly Review Press.

Frank, Andre Gunder. 1967. *Capitalism and Underdevelopment in Latin America.* New York: Monthly Review Press.

Frazier, E. Franklin. 1939. *The Negro Family in the United States.* Chicago: University of Chicago Press.

_____ . 1949. *The Negro in the United States.* New York: Macmillan.

_____ . 1957. *Black Bourgeoisie.* Glencoe, Ill.: Free Press.

_____ . 1957. *Race and Culture Contacts in the Modern World.* New York: Knopf.

Freidman, Andrew L. 1977. *Industry and Labor: Class Struggle at Work and Monopoly Capitalism.* London: Macmillan.

Freud, Sigmund. 1961. *The Future of an Illusion.* Garden City, N.Y.: Anchor.

_____ . 1962. *Civilization and Its Discontents.* New York: W. W. Norton & Company.

Frobel, Folker, Jurgen Heinrichs, and Otto Kreye. 1980. *The New International Division of Labor.* Cambridge: Cambridge University Press.

Fuentes, Annette, and Barbara Ehrenreich. 1983. *Women in the Global Factory.* Boston: South End Press.

Gandy, D. R. 1979. *Marx and History.* Austin and London: University of Texas Press.

Garson, Barbara. 1975. *All the Livelong Day: The Meaning and Demeaning of Routine Work.* New York: Doubleday.

Gartman, David. 1986. *Auto Slavery: The Labor Process in the American Automobile Industry.* New Brunswick, N.J.: Rutgers University Press.

Geschwender, James. 1977. *Class, Race, and Worker Insurgency.* Cambridge: Cambridge University Press.

Gimenez, Martha. 1987. "The Feminization of Poverty: Myth or Reality." *The Insurgent Sociologist* 14, no. 3 (Fall).

Glavanis, Kathy, and Pandeli Glavanis, eds. 1990. *The Rural Middle East*. London: Zed Books.

Glenn, Evelyn Nakano, and Roslyn L. Feldberg. 1977. "Degraded and Deskilled: The Proletarianization of Clerical Work." *Social Problems* 25.

Gold, David, Clarence Y. H. Lo, and Erik Olin Wright. 1975. "Some Recent Developments in Marxist Theories of the Capitalist State," parts 1 and 2. *Monthly Review* 27, nos. 5 and 6 (October and November).

Goldfield, Michael, and Melvin Rothenberg. 1980. *The Myth of Capitalism Reborn: A Marxist Critique of Theories of Capitalist Restoration in the USSR*. San Francisco: Line of March Publications.

Gramsci, Antonio. 1971. *Prison Notebooks*. New York: International Publishers.

_____. 1978. *Selections from Political Writings 1921–26*. London: Lawrence & Wishart.

Green, Gil. 1976. *What's Happening to Labor*. New York: International Publishers.

Green, J. 1980. *The World of the Worker: Labor in Twentieth Century America*. New York: Hill and Wang.

Guarasci, R., and G. Peck. 1987. "Work, Class, and Society: Recent Developments and New Directions in Labor Process Theory." *Review of Radical Political Economics* 19.

Gunnarsson, Christer. 1985. "Development Theory and Third World Industrialization." *Journal of Contemporary Asia* 15, no. 2.

Gurley, John G. 1976. *Challengers to Capitalism*. San Francisco: San Francisco Book Company.

Halliday, Fred. 1979. *Iran: Dictatorship and Development*. New York: Penguin.

Hamilton, Clive. 1983. "Capitalist Industrialization in East Asia's Four Little Tigers." *Journal of Contemporary Asia* 13, no. 1.

_____. 1986. *Capitalist Industrialization in Korea*. Boulder, Colo.: Westview Press.

Hamilton, Nora. 1975. "Mexico: The Limits of State Autonomy." *Latin American Perspectives* 2, no. 2 (Summer).

Hamilton, Richard. 1972. *Class and Politics in the United States*. New York: Wiley.

Harris, Richard, ed. 1975. *The Political Economy of Africa*. Cambridge, Mass.: Schenkman.

Harrison, Bennett, and Barry Bluestone. 1988. *The Great U-Turn: Corporate Restructuring and the Polarizing of America*. New York: Basic Books.

Hart-Landsberg, Martin. 1979. "Export-Led Industrialization in the Third World: Manufacturing Imperialism." *Review of Radical Political Economics* 11, no. 4 (Winter 1979).

_____. 1993. *The Rush To Development*. New York: Monthly Review Press.

Hartman, Heidi. 1976. "Capitalism, Patriarchy and Job Segregation by Sex." *Signs* 1.

Harvey, David. 1982. *The Limits to Capital*. Cambridge, Mass.: Basil Blackwell.

_____. 1989. *The Condition of Postmodernity*. Cambridge, Mass.: Basil Blackwell.

Herman, A. 1982. "Conceptualizing Control: Domination and Hegemony in the Capitalist Labor Process." *The Insurgent Sociologist* 11, no. 3.

Hilton, Rodney, ed. 1976. *The Transition from Feudalism to Capitalism*. London: New Left Books.

Hing, Lo Shiu. 1990. "Political Participation in Hong Kong, South Korea, and Taiwan." *Journal of Contemporary Asia* 20, no. 2.

Hirsh, Joachim. 1979. "The State Apparatus and Social Reproduction: Elements of a Theory of the Bourgeois State." In John Holloway and Sol Picciotto (eds.), *State and Capital: A Marxist Debate*. Austin: University of Texas Press.

Hobsbawm, Eric. 1962. *The Age of Revolution: 1789–1848*. New York: World.

_____ . 1975. *The Age of Capital: 1848–1875*. New York: Scribner's.

Hodges, Donald C., and Robert Elias Abu Shanab, eds. 1972. *NLF: National Liberation Fronts, 1960/1970*. New York: William Morrow & Co.

Holloway, John, and Sol Picciotto. 1977. "Capital, Crisis and the State." *Capital and Class*, no. 2.

Holt, Alix, ed. 1978. *Selected Writings of Alexandra Kollontai*. Westport, Conn.: Lawrence Hill and Company.

Hooglund, Eric. 1982. *Land and Revolution in Iran, 1960–1980*. Austin: University of Texas Press.

Horne, Gerald. 1986. *Black & Red: W.E.B. Du Bois and the Afro-American Response to the Cold War, 1944–1963*. Albany: State University of New York Press.

Hossfeld, Karen J. 1990. " 'Their Logic Against Them': Contradictions in Sex, Race, and Class in Silicon Valley," in Kathryn Ward (ed.), *Women Workers and Global Restructuring*. Ithaca, N.Y.: Cornell University Press.

Howe, Carolyn. 1986. "The Politics of Class Compromise in an International Context: Considerations for a New Strategy for Labor." *Review of Radical Political Economics* 18, no. 3.

Howe, Gary Nigel. 1982. "Dependency Theory, Imperialism, and the Production of Surplus Value on a World Scale," in Ronald H. Chilcote (eds.), *Dependency and Marxism*. Boulder: Westview Press.

Howe, Irving, ed. 1972. *The World of the Blue Collar Worker*. New York: Quadrangle Books.

Hunnius, Gerry, et al., eds. 1973. *Workers' Control: A Reader on Labor and Social Change*. New York: Vintage.

Hunter, Floyd. 1953. *Community Power Structure*. Chapel Hill: University of North Carolina Press.

_____ . 1959. *Top Leadership U.S.A.* Chapel Hill: University of North Carolina Press.

Hussain, Mahmoud. 1973. *Class Conflict in Egypt, 1945–1970*. New York: Monthly Review Press.

Inalcik, Halil. 1973. *The Ottoman Empire*. New York: Praeger.

Issawi, Charles, ed. 1966. *The Economic History of the Middle East*. Chicago: University of Chicago Press.

Jay, Martin. 1973. *The Dialectical Imagination*. Boston: Little, Brown and Company.

Jayawardena, Kumari. 1986. *Feminism and Nationalism in the Third World*. London: Zed Books.

Jelin, Elizabeth, ed. 1990. *Women and Social Change in Latin America*. London: Zed Books.

Jenkins, Rhys. 1987. *Transnational Corporations and Uneven Development*. New York: Methuen.

Jessop, Bob. 1982. *The Capitalist State*. New York: New York University Press.

Katznelson, Ira, and Al Zolberg, eds. 1986. *Working Class Formation: Nineteenth-century Patterns in Western Europe and the United States*. Princeton, N.J.: Princeton University Press.

Keeran, Roger. 1980. *The Communist Party and the Auto Workers' Unions*. Bloomington, Ind.: Indiana University Press.

Keyder, Caglar. 1987. *State and Class in Turkey*. London: Verso.

Kitano, Harry, and Roger Daniels. 1988. *Asian Americans: Emerging Minorities*. Englewood Cliffs, N.J.: Prentice Hall.

Kloby, Jerry. 1993. "Increasing Class Polarization in the United States: The Growth of Wealth and Income Inequality," in Berch Berberoglu (ed.), *Critical Perspectives in Sociology: A Reader*, 2d ed. Dubuque, Iowa: Kendall/Hunt Publishing Company.

Knapp, Peter, and Alan J. Spector. 1991. *Crisis and Change: Basic Questions of Marxist Sociology*. Chicago: Nelson-Hall Publishers.

Kollontai, Alexandra. 1978. "Sexual Relations and the Class Struggle," in Alix Holt (ed.), *Selected Writings of Alexandra Kollontai*. Westport, Conn.: Lawrence Hill and Company.

_____ . 1978. "The Social Basis of the Woman Question," in Alix Holt (ed.), *Selected Writings of Alexandra Kollontai*. Westport, Conn.: Lawrence Hill and Company.

Krader, Lawrence. 1975. *The Asiatic Mode of Production*. Assen: Van Gorcum.

Laclau, Ernesto. 1971. "Feudalism and Capitalism in Latin America." *New Left Review* 67 (May-June).

Landsberg, Martin. 1979. "Export-Led Industrialization in the Third World: Manufacturing Imperialism." *Review of Radical Political Economics* 11, no. 4 (Winter).

Leacock, Eleanor B. 1972. "Introduction," to F. Engels, *The Origin of the Family, Private Property, and the State*. New York: International Publishers.

Leggett, John C. 1991. *Mining the Fields: Farm Workers Fight Back*. Highland Park, N.J.: The Raritan Institute.

Lembcke, Jerry. 1988. *Capitalist Development and Class Capacities: Marxist Theory and Union Organization*. Westport, Conn.: Greenwood Press.

Lenin, V. I. 1947. *Works*. Vol. 31. Moscow: Foreign Languages Publishing House.

_____ . 1971. *Imperialism, The Highest Stage of Capitalism*. In V. I. Lenin, *Selected Works*. New York: International Publishers.

_____ . 1971. *The State and Revolution*. In V. I. Lenin, *Selected Works in One Volume*. New York: International Publishers.

_____ . 1971. *What Is To Be Done?* In V. I. Lenin, *Selected Works*. New York: International Publishers.

_____ . 1974. *On Historical Materialism*. New York: International Publishers.

_____ . 1975. *Selected Works in Three Volumes*. Vol. 2. Moscow: Progress Publishers.

Lenski, Gerhard. 1966. *Power and Privilege*. New York: McGraw-Hill.

Levine, Rhonda. 1988. *Class Struggle and the New Deal: Industrial Labor, Industrial Capital, and the State*. Lawrence, Kans.: University Press of Kansas.

Levkovsky, A. I. 1966. *Capitalism in India*. Delhi: People's Publishing House.

Leys, Colin. 1975. *Underdevelopment in Kenya*. Berkeley: University of California Press.

Limqueco, Peter, and Bruce McFarlane, eds. 1983. *Neo-Marxist Theories of Development*. London: Croom Helm; New York: St. Martin's Press.

Longuenesse, Elizabeth. 1979. "The Class Nature of the State in Syria." *MERIP Reports* 9, no. 4 (May).

Loren, Charles. 1977. *Classes in the United States*. Davis, Calif.: Cardinal Publishers.

Luxemburg, Rosa. 1913. *The Accumulation of Capital*. Reprint. New Haven: Yale University Press, 1951.

Mafeje, A. 1977. "Neo-colonialism, State Capitalism, or Revolution?" in P.C.W. Gutkind and P. Waterman (eds.), *African Social Studies*. London: Heinemann.

Mamdani, Mahmood. 1976. *Politics and Class Formation in Uganda*. New York: Monthly Review Press.

Mandel, Ernest. 1975. *Late Capitalism*. London: New Left Books.

―――. 1979. *From Class Society to Communism*. London: Ink Links.

―――. 1980. *The Second Slump*. London: Verso.

Marable, Manning. 1986. *W.E.B. Du Bois: Black Radical Democrat*. Boston: Twayne Publishers.

Marcus, Tessa. 1990. *Modernizing Super-Exploitation*. London: Zed Books.

Marcy, Sam. 1977. *The Class Character of the USSR*. New York: World View Publishers.

Marger, Martin N. 1987. *Elites and Masses: An Introduction to Political Sociology*. 2d ed. Belmont, Calif.: Wadsworth.

Markakis, John. 1990. *National and Class Conflict in the Horn of Africa*. London: Zed Books.

Marquit, Erwin. 1978. *The Socialist Countries*. Minneapolis: MEP Publications.

Marx, Karl. 1962. *Capital*. 3 vols. Moscow: Foreign Languages Publishing House.

―――. 1964. *Selected Writings in Sociology and Social Philosophy*. New York: McGraw-Hill.

―――. 1965. *Pre-Capitalist Economic Formations*. New York: International Publishers.

―――. 1972. *The Eighteenth Brumaire of Louis Bonaparte*. In Karl Marx and Frederick Engels, *Selected Works*. New York: International Publishers.

―――. 1972. *The Civil War in France*. In Karl Marx and Frederick Engels, *Selected Works*. New York: International Publishers.

―――. 1972. *Critique of the Gotha Program*. In Karl Marx and Frederick Engels, *Selected Works*. New York: International Publishers.

―――. 1972. *Preface to a Contribution to the Critique of Political Economy*. In Karl Marx and Frederick Engels, *Selected Works*. New York: International Publishers.

Marx, K., and F. Engels. 1947. *The German Ideology*. New York: International Publishers.

―――. 1972. *Manifesto of the Communist Party*. In Karl Marx and Frederick Engels, *Selected Works*. New York: International Publishers.

Mayorga, Rene Antonio. 1978. "National-Popular State, State Capitalism, and Military Dictatorship." *Latin American Perspectives* 5, no. 2 (Spring).

McMichael, Philip, James Petras, and Robert Rhodes. 1974. "Imperialism and the Contradictions of Development," *New Left Review*, no. 85 (May-June).

McNall, Scott, Rhonda Levine, and Rick Fantasia, eds. 1991. *Bringing Class Back In*. Boulder: Westview Press.

McWilliams, Carey. 1971. *Factories in the Field*. Santa Barbara and Salt Lake City: Peregrine Publishers.

Melman, S. 1970. *Pentagon Capitalism: The Political Economy of War*. New York: McGraw-Hill.

Melman, Seymour. 1965. *Our Depleted Society*. New York: Holt, Rinehart and Winston.

Merton, Robert K. 1968. *Social Theory and Social Structure*. New York: Free Press.

Michels, Robert. 1968. *Political Parties*. New York: Free Press.

Mies, Maria. 1986. *Patriarchy and Accumulation on a World Scale: Women in the International Division of Labor*. London: Zed Books.

Miliband, Ralph. 1969. *The State in Capitalist Society*. New York: Basic Books.

———. 1975. "Political Forms and Historical Materialism," in R. Miliband and J. Saville (eds.), *Socialist Register, 1975*. London: Merlin Press.

———. 1977. *Marxism and Politics*. London: Oxford University Press.

———. 1982. *Capitalist Democracy in Britain*. London: Oxford University Press.

———. 1989. *Divided Societies: Class Struggle in Contemporary Capitalism*. Oxford: Clarendon Press.

Milkman, Ruth. 1987. *Gender at Work*. Urbana: University of Illinois Press.

Miller, Norman, and Roderick Aya, eds. 1971. *National Liberation: Revolution in the Third World*. New York: Free Press.

Mills, C. Wright. 1951. *White Collar: The American Middle Classes*. New York: Oxford University Press.

———. 1956. *The Power Elite*. New York: Oxford University Press.

———. 1959. *The Sociological Imagination*. New York: Oxford University Press.

———. 1963. "The Structure of Power in American Society," in *Power, Politics, and People: The Collected Essays of C. Wright Mills*, ed. Irving Louis Horowitz. New York: Oxford University Press.

Mohiddin, Ahmed. 1981. *African Socialism in Two Countries*. London: Croom Helm.

Mollenkopf, John. 1975. "Theories of the State and Power Structure Research." *Insurgent Sociologist* 5, no. 3.

Montgomery, David. 1976. "Workers' Control of Machine Production in the Nineteenth Century." *Labor History* 17, no. 4.

Moody, Kim. 1988. *An Injury to All: The Decline of American Unionism*. London: Verso.

Moore, Barrington, Jr. 1968. *The Social Origins of Democracy and Dictatorship*. London: Penguin.

Morais, Herbert M. 1944. *The Struggle for American Freedom*. New York: International Publishers.

Mosca, Gaetano. 1939. *The Ruling Class*. New York: McGraw-Hill.

Moulder, Frances V. 1977. *Japan, China and the Modern World Economy*. Cambridge: Cambridge University Press.

Munck, Ronaldo. 1984. *Politics and Dependency in the Third World*. London: Zed Books.

———. 1990. *Latin America: The Transition to Democracy*. London: Zed Books.

Nash, June, and Maria Patricia Fernandez-Kelly, eds. 1983. *Women, Men, and the International Division of Labor*. Albany: State University of New York Press.

Nichols, Theo, and Huw Beynon. 1977. *Living with Capitalism: Class Relations and the Modern Factory*. London: Routledge & Kegan Paul.

Nicolaus, Martin. 1975. *Restoration of Capitalism in the USSR*. Chicago: Liberator Press.

Nissen, Bruce. 1981. "U.S. Workers and the U.S. Labor Movement." *Monthly Review* 33, no. 1 (May).

O'Connor, James. 1984. *Accumulation Crisis*. New York: Basil Blackwell.

Odeh, B. J. 1985. *Lebanon: Dynamics of Conflict*. London: Zed Press.

Ollman, Bertell. 1987. "How to Study Class Consciousness and Why We Should." *Critical Sociology* 14, no. 1 (Winter).

Olson, W. 1985. "Crisis and Social Change in Mexico's Political Economy." *Latin American Perspectives* 46.

Onimode, Bade. 1985. *An Introduction to Marxist Political Economy*. London: Zed Books.

———. 1989. *A Political Economy of the African Crisis*. London: Zed Books.

Parenti, Michael. 1988. *Democracy for the Few*. 5th ed. New York: St. Martin's Press.

Pareto, Vilfredo. 1935. *The Mind and Society*. 4 vols. Edited by Arthur Livingstone. New York: Harcourt, Brace and Company.

Parsons, Talcott. 1951. *The Social System*. New York: Free Press.

———. 1960. *Structure and Process in Modern Societies*. New York: Free Press.

———. 1966. *Societies: An Evolutionary Approach*. Englewood Cliffs, N.J.: Prentice-Hall.

Peet, Richard, ed. 1987. *International Capitalism and Industrial Restructuring*. Boston: Allen & Unwin.

Perlo, Victor. 1988. *Super Profits and Crises: Modern U.S. Capitalism*. New York: International Publishers.

Petras, James F. 1978. *Critical Perspectives on Imperialism and Social Class in the Third World*. New York: Monthly Review Press.

———. 1981. *Class, State and Power in the Third World*. Montclair, N.J.: Allanheld, Osmun.

———. 1983. *Capitalist and Socialist Crises in the Late Twentieth Century*. Totowa, N.J.: Rowman & Allanheld.

Petras, James, and Christian Bay. 1990. "The Changing Wealth of the U.S. Ruling Class." *Monthly Review* 42, no. 7 (December).

Pfeffer, Richard M. 1979. *Working for Capitalism*. New York: Columbia University Press.

Piven, Frances Fox, and Richard Cloward. 1982. *The New Class War*. New York: Pantheon.

Platt, Anthony M. 1991. *E. Franklin Frazier Reconsidered*. New Brunswick, N.J.: Rutgers University Press.

Poulantzas, Nicos. 1974. *Political Power and Social Classes*. London: New Left Books.

———. 1975. *Classes in Contemporary Capitalism*. London: New Left Books.

———. 1978. *State, Power, Socialism*. London: New Left Books.

Quijano, Anibal. 1971. *Nationalism and Capitalism in Peru*. New York: Modern Reader.

Rahman, Atiur. 1987. *Peasants and Classes*. London: Zed Books.

Reich, Wilhelm. 1970. *The Mass Psychology of Fascism*. New York: Farrar, Straus & Giroux.

Roos, Patricia. 1981. "Sexual Stratification in the Workplace: Male-Female Differences in Economic Returns to Occupation." *Social Science Research* 10.

Ross, Robert J. S., and Kent C. Trachte. 1990. *Global Capitalism: The New Leviathan*. Albany: State University of New York Press.

Rowbotham, Sheila. 1972. *Women, Resistance, and Revolution*. New York: Penguin.

Safa, Helen I. 1986. "Runaway Shops and Female Employment: The Search for Cheap Labor," in Eleanor Leacock and Helen I. Safa (eds.), *Women's Work*. South Hadley, Mass.: Bergin and Garvey.

Salt, James. 1989. "Sunbelt Capital and Conservative Political Realignment in the 1970s and 1980s." *Critical Sociology* 16, no. 2–3 (Summer-Fall).

Sattel, Jack. 1978. "The Degradation of Labor in the Twentieth Century: Harry Braverman's Sociology of Work." *The Insurgent Sociologist* 8, no. 1 (Winter).

Sayigh, Rosemary. 1979. *Palestinians: From Peasants to Revolutionaries*. London: Zed Press.

Sen, Anupam. 1982. *The State, Industrialization, and Class Formations in India*. London: Routledge & Kegan Paul.

Sender, John, and Sheila Smith. 1986. *The Development of Capitalism in Africa*. London: Methuen & Co.

Shaiken, Harley. 1986. *Work Transformed: Automation and Labor in the Computer Age*. Lexington, Mass.: Lexington Books.

Shivji, Issa G. 1976. *Class Struggles in Tanzania*. New York: Monthly Review Press.

_____. 1986. *The State and the Working People in Tanzania*. Dakar: CODESRIA.

Sinha, Arun. 1990. *Against the Few: Struggles of India's Rural Poor*. London: Zed Books.

Sklair, Leslie. 1989. *Assembling for Development: The Maquila Industry in Mexico and the United States*. Boston: Unwin Hyman.

Skocpol, Theda. 1979. *States and Revolutions: A Comparative Analysis of France, Russia and China*. Cambridge: Cambridge University Press.

Slaughter, Jane. 1990. "Is the Labor Movement Reaching a Turning Point?" *Labor Notes*, no. 130 (January).

Smith, Sheila. 1982. "Class Analysis Versus World System: Critique of Samir Amin's Typology of Underdevelopment." *Journal of Contemporary Asia* 12, no. 1.

Smith, Tony. 1990. *The Logic of Marx's Capital*. Albany: State University of New York Press.

Snow, Robert T. 1983. "The New International Division of Labor and the U.S. Work Force: The Case of the Electronics Industry," in June Nash and Maria Patricia Fernandez-Kelly (eds.), *Women, Men and the International Division of Labor*. Albany: State University of New York Press.

So, Alvin Y., 1990. "How to Conduct Class Analysis in the World Economy?" *Sociological Perspectives* 33.

So, Alvin Y., and Suwarsono. 1990. "Class Theory or Class Analysis? A Reexamination of Marx's Unfinished Chapter on Class." *Critical Sociology* 17, no. 2 (Summer).

Stein, Stanley J., and Barbara H. Stein. 1970. *The Colonial Heritage of Latin America*. New York: Oxford University Press.

Stepan-Norris, Judith, and Maurice Zeitlin. 1989. " 'Who Gets the Bird?' or, How the Communists Won Power in America's Unions." *American Sociological Review* 54 (August 1989).

Stinchcombe, Arthur L. 1963. "Some Empirical Consequences of the Davis-Moore Theory of Stratification." *American Sociological Review* 28, no. 5 (October).

Stork, Joe. 1989. "Class, State, and Politics in Iraq," in Berch Berberoglu (ed.), *Power and Stability in the Middle East*. London: Zed Books.

Sweezy, Paul M. 1942. *The Theory of Capitalist Development*. New York: Monthly Review Press.

Sweezy, Paul M., and Charles Bettelheim, eds. 1971. *On the Transition to Socialism*. New York: Monthly Review Press.

Szymanski, Albert. 1978. *The Capitalist State and the Politics of Class*. Cambridge, Mass.: Winthrop.

———. 1979. *Is the Red Flag Flying? The Political Economy of the Soviet Union*. London: Zed Press.

———. 1981. *The Logic of Imperialism*. New York: Praeger.

———. 1983. *Class Structure: A Critical Perspective*. New York: Praeger.

Tabb, William K. 1989. "Capital Mobility, The Restructuring of Production, and the Politics of Labor," in Arthur MacEwan and William K. Tabb (eds.), *Instability and Change in the World Economy*. New York: Monthly Review Press.

Therborn, Goran. 1976. *Science, Class and Society*. London: New Left Books.

———. 1978. *What Does the Ruling Class Do When It Rules?* London: New Left Books.

———. 1980. *The Ideology of Power and the Power of Ideology*. London: New Left Books.

Thompson, E. P. 1963. *The Making of the English Working Class*. New York: Pantheon.

Tumin, Melvin. 1953. "Some Principles of Stratification: A Critical Analysis." *American Sociological Review* 18, no. 4 (August).

———. 1953. "Reply to Kingsley Davis." *American Sociological Review* 18, no. 6 (December).

Vickers, Jeanne. 1991. *Women and the World Economic Crisis*. London: Zed Books.

Waas, Michael Van. 1982. "Multinational Corporations and the Politics of Labor Supply." *The Insurgent Sociologist* 11, No. 3.

Wallerstein, Immanuel. 1974. *The Modern World System*. New York: Academic Press.

———. 1979. *The Capitalist World Economy*. Cambridge: Cambridge University Press.

———. 1984. *The Politics of the World Economy*. Cambridge: Cambridge University Press.

Ward, Kathryn, ed. 1990. *Women Workers and Global Restructuring*. Ithaca, N.Y.: Cornell University Press.

Warren, Bill. 1973. "Imperialism and Capitalist Industrialization." *New Left Review* no. 81 (September-October).

———. 1980. *Imperialism, Pioneer of Capitalism*. London: Verso.

Weber, Max. 1948. *The Protestant Ethic and the Spirit of Capitalism*. New York: Scribner's.

———. 1964. *The Theory of Social and Economic Organization*. Edited and with an introduction by Talcott Parsons. New York: Free Press.

———. 1967. *From Max Weber. Essays in Sociology*. Translated, edited, and with an introduction by H. H. Gerth and C. Wright Mills. New York: Oxford University Press.

_____ . 1968. *Economy and Society*. 3 vols. New York: Bedminster Press.

Weeks, John. 1981. *Capital and Exploitation*. Princeton: Princeton University Press.

Weinberg, Meyer, ed. 1970. *W.E.B. Du Bois: A Reader*. New York: Harper & Row.

Williams, Eric. 1966. *Capitalism and Slavery*. New York: Capricorn.

Willie, Charles V., ed. 1989. *The Caste and Class Controversy on Race and Poverty*. Dix Hills, N.Y.: General Hall.

Wilson, William Julius. 1978. *The Declining Significance of Race*. Chicago: University of Chicago Press.

_____ . 1987. *The Truly Disadvantaged: The Inner City, the Underclass, and Public Policy*. Chicago: University of Chicago Press.

Wood, Stephen, ed. 1982. *The Degradation of Work? Skill, Deskilling, and the Labor Process*. London: Hutchinson and Company.

_____ . 1989. *The Transformation of Work?* London: Unwin Hyman.

Wright, Erik Olin. 1976. "Class Boundaries in Advanced Capitalist Societies." *New Left Review*, no. 98.

_____ . 1978. *Class, Crisis and the State*. London: New Left Books.

_____ . 1980. "Varieties of Marxist Conceptions of Class Structure." *Politics and Society* 9, no. 3.

_____ . 1985. *Classes*. London: Verso.

_____ . 1989. *The Debate on Classes*. London: Verso.

Zaalouk, Malak. 1989. *Power, Class and Foreign Capital in Egypt*. London: Zed Books.

Zeitlin, Maurice. 1980. *Classes, Class Conflict, and the State*. Cambridge, Mass.: Winthrop.

Index

About the Author

BERCH BERBEROGLU is Professor and Chairman of the Department of Sociology and Director of the Institute for International Studies at the University of Nevada, Reno. Dr. Berberoglu has written or edited 14 books including *The Legacy of Empire: Economic Decline and Class Polarization in the United States* (Praeger, 1992), *The Labor Process and Control of Labor: The Changing Nature of Work Relations in the Late Twentieth Century* (Praeger, 1993), and *The Internationalization of Capital: Imperialism and Capitalist Development on a World Scale* (Praeger, 1987).

ISBN 0-275-94924-9

EAN

9 780275 949242

HARDCOVER BAR CODE

90000>